Creeping up on Auckland

To my daughter Miranda,
who wanted to know about it

Creeping up on Auckland

C. A. LATIMER

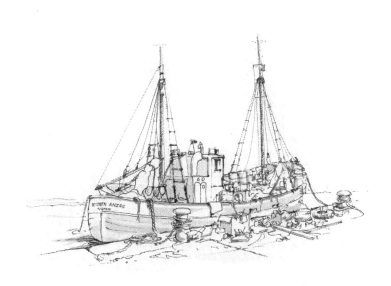

SEAFARER BOOKS

Creeping Up on Auckland first published 2003

© C. A. Latimer

This edition published in 2005 by
Seafarer Books
102 Redwald Road
Rendlesham
Woodbridge
Suffolk IP12 2TE
www.seafarerbooks.com

ISBN   0 9547062 2 6

A CIP catalogue record for this book is available from the British Library

Edited by Hugh Brazier
Typesetting and design by Julie Rainford
Cover design by Louis Mackay
Drawings by John Roberts
Photographs from Courtenay Latimer's personal archive

Printed in Finland by WS Bookwell OY

CONTENTS

PREFACE

In 2002 I asked my daughter Miranda what she would like for Christmas. She said she wanted to read the full story of the passage I made to New Zealand in 1959–60. I had sometimes referred to it, and she had met a couple of the other crew members when they made visits to our house, but she wanted a proper joined-up account of the episode.

I soon realised when I started writing the tale for her that an ocean passage 45 years ago had many characteristics which do not obtain in the twenty-first century, and that is why I have added a glossary. We lived in such a different world that this account is, in part, a window into the nautical past, with usages and equipment which seem absurd today. In order to preserve the historical framework I have also kept the place names that were in use at the time, although I am well aware that many of them have changed.

Health and safety played little part aboard the *Aberdeen Anzac*, not because we were unusually insouciant but because those matters were not given much attention 45 years ago. Nor, I should add, was much consideration given to diet.

The extent to which the places on our route have changed was brought home to me when I remembered that on the Galapagos and the Marquesas we did not encounter a single tourist. Remoteness ruled.

My source material, although scanty, includes a ragged and salt-stained notebook in which I made notes, optimistically hoping that they would prod my memory – as for example reminding me of certain events which might otherwise have been forgotten, such as someone's birthday. The story as it was originally written for my daughter was published in 2003, but since then some more information has come to light, prompting this new Seafarer Books edition, with glossary, and drawings by John Roberts, a Woodbridge friend and artist – who has a feeling for boats and the strangely rare ability to draw them.

C. A. Latimer
September 2005

CREEPING UP ON AUCKLAND

THE EVENTS leading up to our passage to New Zealand aboard the 70-foot Motor Fishing Vessel *Aberdeen Anzac* were various and complicated – a game of snakes and ladders, forwards and backwards; a story of mistakes and delays. Our (that is, Les and I; more about Les later) original plan had been to sail to the Antipodes in the Brixham trawler *Gratitude*. She had been built by the Jackman Brothers of Brixham in 1907, and was not in good condition. She would never have got there and would probably have drowned us in the attempt. The guardian angel who, in retrospect, seems to have watched over the whole project from beginning to end evidently started work in the summer of 1957 when *Gratitude*, having had her rudder removed during her refit, was towed into the wall of the Wellington Dock at Dover and seriously damaged. Her bowsprit had not been housed, but stood out about fifteen feet beyond her stem-head. When she ran into the dock, this great battering ram of solid wood ran back, smashing into the metal water tank in front of the saloon coach roof and carrying it into the saloon, a mess of collapsed metal, depositing about fifty gallons of water onto the saloon table. We made a successful claim against the tug company, and temporarily shelved our plans. I went to live at Woodbridge in Suffolk to take up a job as a yacht broker, while Les stayed in Sandwich, near Dover, to sell the remains of *Gratitude* and find another boat. His partner, Pam, had trained as a chemist and was able to find a good job in the laboratory of the Pfizer factory nearby.

Nearly two years went by, and I would have been ready to abandon the project but Les, to his credit, never wavered in his ambition to take a small boat either to Australia or to New Zealand. He knew next to nothing about sailing, navigation or the sea in general, but he was Australian and I have observed that they are a people who are undaunted by their own ignorance and feel that, in spite of all evidence to the contrary, nothing is beyond them. In consequence, they often succeed where the more prudent will either fail or never start in the first place. It is an attractive trait, but it can get their associates into trouble. I had been alerted to Les's ignorance when, with the chart spread on the cabin table, he had pointed to the land area and referred to the heights shown in such a way as to make it clear that he thought they were sea soundings. He wasn't joking. I decided that I would depend on my own limited knowledge for any navigational decisions. For my part, I had my full quota of foolish optimism and delusions of competence, but I had some experience of yachting on a 20-ton cutter in Scotland, and was a little more aware of the dangers of a long ocean passage in a badly prepared boat. I had not yet been thoroughly frightened and so had not reached the healthy outlook of 'He who has suffered Shipwracke fears to saile Upon the seas, though with a gentle gale' (Robert Herrick). Les and I had messed about with *Gratitude* in the Channel, but we had been lucky, and although we had hit the hard sand of the Dutch coast a couple of serious thumps, nothing had happened to unnerve us.

* * * * *

In 1959 I was being hard worked as a yacht broker. I went down from time to time to see Les and Pam, and to assure him that if and when he found another boat, I was ready to put up my share of the cost and join him in another attempt. I couldn't play much part in the search, except insofar as I could send him details of any craft which came onto our books for sale which seemed suitable. Les found a small fishing-boat conversion which he bought as a speculation, a delightful 40-foot Scottish boat which we brought down from Whitby to the Southwick Canal near Brighton in the Easter of 1959, but she was immediately put up for sale – she was too small for us. He sold her, eventually, at a profit, and put the money aside for the larger boat which he hoped to find. This presented itself in the form of the 70-foot Admiralty type Motor Fishing Vessel *Whinnyfold*. I sent Les the details, but he had already spotted her in a private advertisement. He bought her, and the first thing he did was to change her name to *Aberdeen Anzac*. Nobody regretted the disappearance of *Whinnyfold*. He and Pam then started the process of gathering together a crew. Apart from the three of us, we needed nine others, who were acquired by advertisement in the *Observer*. An enormous number of applicants was carefully sifted – Pam wrote the letters – and eventually, by the autumn of 1959, we had our full complement of 12. Each was asked to put in some cash to pay for the costs of fuel, food and the other inevitable expenses of a 12,000 mile passage. I scraped together what I could, which included my share of the sale of *Gratitude* (Les had sold her well, in spite of her sorry state), while Pam put in the largest share, having sold her cottage in Sandwich.

That summer of 1959 had been one of the driest and hottest in memory, and it was just starting to break up as I drove down to Southwick with our engineer, Dick, whose job it would be to look after *Aberdeen Anzac*'s 160-horsepower Lister Blackstone diesel. I'm not sure what his experience had been, but he seemed both confident and competent: a laconic 27-year-old. I was quite happy that he should rule in the engine room, not a place where I planned to spend much time. When we arrived at the

Southwick Canal, most of the crew had already assembled, and we all had a meal together in the saloon of *Boomerang*, the small boat which Les had just sold. We sat around the table eating a large beef and rice dinner. Rice: that was a portent for the future. It has always struck me that it is entirely arbitrary, what one remembers and forgets. I remember that meal with complete clarity. It was the first time I had met my shipmates, and they were a very diverse group.

Tim, in his early forties, was our radio expert. He had been a radio officer in the RAF during the war, had served on air–sea rescue powerboats, acquiring some nautical knowledge, and was also knowledgeable about the engine room. Keith, 27, who had signed on as an engineer, was a PhD from Sheffield University who had worked at Harwell, which had given him a slightly sinister mystique. He had put in a substantial sum towards the venture. George and Muriel, in their early forties, were a married couple, both schoolteachers, who were going to find jobs in New Zealand: George had been in the Navy for many years, and Muriel had trained as a nurse. Bill, also about 40, had been working with 'punch cards', and although I had dozens of conversations with him, coming to know him well, I never really found out what he did. I think he found it impossible to explain to me – I was, as we would say now, 'too far behind'. Nigel, 33, was an Australian who had been living and working in England and was now returning to his beloved Queensland. He had very recently married an English girl who was going out to Australia by more orthodox means. He had signed on as an electrician, and that he certainly was, but we also found that he was a first-rate carpenter as well, an accomplishment which was going to prove valuable in the coming months. Dave, 30, was a trawlerman, but he too had other skills which became apparent later. He looked the very model of a trawlerman, in his speckled sweater, cloth cap and extremely powerful frame. He inspired great confidence when seen about the deck, handling heavy warps as if they were pieces of string.

I have left Jim to the end because he was, as it were, a bonus. He was also, I believe, placed on *Aberdeen Anzac* by that guardian angel that I mentioned earlier. He wasn't originally meant to be in our crew, but he lived at that time in Southwick, and had come aboard out of curiosity when he heard about our plans. His parents lived nearby and he was briefly at a loose end having recently sat, and passed, his examination by the Board of Trade as Master Mariner. Twenty-seven years old, he had been at sea in the British India Steam Navigation Company since joining as a cadet at about 16; he had therefore gained his Master's ticket in the shortest time possible. At first, it puzzled me – why did he, who clearly had a promising career at sea ahead of him, want to waste his time on our ramshackle project? Later, when I knew him better, it became clearer, but that is to anticipate.

This, then, was our ship's company, and having met them I felt cheered and left the next morning to take my car up to my mother's home in Cumberland, to lay it up until such time as I would collect it again on my return to England. I had no plans to stay in New Zealand. When I returned to Southwick by train, *Aberdeen Anzac* was nearing readiness for departure. She was in chaos, taking on stores, engine spares – everything she needed for her voyage. She had been built by Forbes of Peterhead in 1946. Her history was obscure as it was not at all clear what she had been doing for the previous thirteen years. She had obviously been travelling a good deal, unless her engine had been put into her when it had already been well used, but it seemed that she had not spent much time fishing because she had no evidence of ever having had fish in her – no fishy smell or fish scales in her bilges. But her seine net winch was well used. It is possible that she had been in Admiralty service, but there was no information about that or any record of such use. She was 70 feet overall, about 65 feet on the waterline, with a beam of 19 feet and draft of 9 feet. A good solid substantial vessel, which as events turned out she certainly needed to be. Les had chosen well, and as I walked round her deck, looking at her arrangements and fittings, I was pleased that she should be our transport.

In other respects, however, our prospects were not so encouraging. She was pitifully poorly equipped for a long passage, because we had no money to spare for anything more than the barest essentials. We had three sextants on board – Les's, Jim's and mine – but no chronometer, until Les 'borrowed' one from another boat in the Southwick Canal. That is what I understood from shipboard rumour, and I made a point of never asking him where he had got it. I didn't want to know; Les was my partner and I wanted to keep the relationship simple. The engine room, so far as we could tell, was a fairly sound area, with the standard Lister Blackstone diesel, started by air bottles which were in their turn charged by a 14-horsepower compressor. This was mounted beside the main engine and was started by hand, a muscular chore involving two men, unless it was Dave. The fuel tanks had a capacity of 1,700 gallons, and Tim had estimated that we would burn 3½ gallons per hour at our usual cruising revolutions. He confirmed this over the coming days by carefully monitoring our consumption. Allowing a safe margin, this indicated that we would have to sail part of the way carrying some reserve fuel in drums on deck.

Our radio equipment was rudimentary. Tim had managed to acquire an emergency air–sea rescue device left over from the war, a yellow object that had apparently been part of the equipment in an aircraft's rubber life raft. It had a handle which, when aircrew found themselves 'in the drink', they would wind to indicate their plight and position. He had also purchased, at a very low cost, an old army tank radio which, although it was illegal for sea use, could receive broadcasts of time signals for navigational use (this was essential) and was also a great blessing in that it was possible to hear *The Archers* until about halfway across the Atlantic. This was very important to Muriel and Pam. Apart from this, all I ever heard from it were crackles, save on one memorable occasion when it gave a short burst of music off the coast of Africa.

Our ground tackle comprised a 112 lb CQR plough anchor, plus a huge and quite useless fisherman anchor of about 300 lb weight, which lurked undisturbed under the ship's boat secured on chocks under the mizzen boom. Not even Dave could shift that great brute; it never moved throughout the voyage. We had sufficient chain for our CQR, and that is what we used on all occasions. We didn't have an anchor winch, but used the trawl winch.

The problem which concerned me most was the need to make AA sail. I had not seen her underwater shape, so could not predict how easily she could be driven through the water, but driven she would have to be. Les had already arranged and had fitted a pair of staysails on booms which attached to the mainmast. These would be tested in due course, and I would also have to make some arrangements to hang some sails on the mizzen mast: every little scrap would help. Sailing would have to wait until we reached the trade-wind area, so I planned to make final arrangements in the Canary Islands. In Southwick, I was uneasy, imagining AA wallowing in the Atlantic for weeks while we ate our way through our meagre stores.

AA had been partitioned to accommodate the twelve of us. In the aft cabin, the principal sleeping and eating space, there were six fixed berths, ranged against the hull around a central area occupied by a large folding table. At the aft end, propped up and facing forward, was a large safe into which all valuables were put, and I can't remember who had the key. In this cabin slept Tim, Dick, Nigel, Keith, Bill and Dave. There was a solid-fuel stove in there too, which kept the place snug in cold weather. Forward of this cabin was the engine room, with the galley above and, approached by a separate door on deck, the WC. Forward of the galley, but at a higher level, was the wheelhouse, to which one mounted from the deck by a steel step to doors either side. The galley and wheelhouse formed part of the whole deck structure and on the port side there was a steel divided door (like a stable door) which was the entrance, leading down a steel ladder to the engine room. In front of the wheelhouse was the winch gear for fishing, aft of the main hatch. Inside the hatch was a shelf which housed the chronometer, and a companionway leading down to the two double cabins for our two couples.

General Arrangement below deck

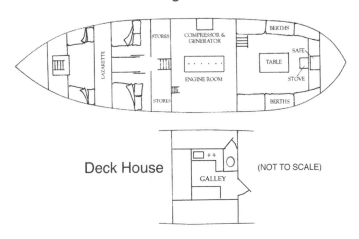

This area was separated by a full bulkhead from the lazarette, a dark food store, running the full width of the boat and about six feet long; this also had a forward bulkhead with a hatch in it to allow access from the fo'c'sle, where Jim and I had our cabin. He slept in a bunk over the sail locker; I had a pipe cot hanging on chains to starboard. We had our own access to the deck by a steel ladder and hatch, and an Elsan toilet, but we never used it. The arrangements in the fo'c'sle were spartan, but the space was generous and, being under the sheer of the bow, headroom was ample. The disadvantage was that the up and down motion in a seaway was enormous, giving me in the early days crazy dreams of bounding along a street like a Springheel Jack, reaching second-floor windows at each stride.

I have described the layout of AA in some detail not because there is anything intrinsically interesting about the accommodation of a North Sea trawler, but because this was to be our home for the next ten months, where we lived, moved and had our being, playing the same part in the story as a stage-set plays in a theatrical production.

Our cooking arrangements were simple, and the division of duties in the galley was typical of a pre-feminist age. Pam and Muriel would take it in turns, day and day about, to be in charge of the galley, helped by one man, on a roster – that is, everyone except Les. As time went by, various people took up particular galley activities. I started making porridge at some point, for example. Cooking was by Calor gas, from two huge 98 lb cylinders stowed in the WC compartment. There was a large hatch from the galley to the wheelhouse, through which cups of coffee could be passed.

Southwick was not a cheerful place to be in late October, and we were all keen to get away. There was a pub, the Sea House, where we went to get a drink, but that was our only resource. It rained frequently, which had the merit of washing the dirt off the deck, but no other advantage, and it was a great relief when towards the end of the month we moved across to the fuelling jetty to fill our tanks with diesel. We were as ready as we were ever going to be, and departed for Dartmouth at the beginning of November, into a grey tossy sea. Jim and I had agreed that while we were coasting, he and I would work alternate watches, six hours on and six off; and after an uneventful passage we arrived in the Dart estuary, tying up at the old coaling jetty on the Kingswear side, near the railway station. We had intended to stay only one night, but the weather forecast was so bad that we decided to wait for a break. There was no break, and we were in Dartmouth for a week, a wretched time of continual rain, with a strong sou'westerly blowing up the Channel. The driving rain and wind splattered and whistled through the streets of the town, and I remember on one typical day as I walked by W. H. Smith's I saw an elegant naval lieutenant coming out of the shop with *The Times* under his arm. It was an old school friend, Bunny Barker, and I nearly shouted 'Bunny!', but stopped myself because I was unshaven and tramp-like, feeling that he would be embarrassed, which was stupid because he wouldn't have been. He was on the staff of the Royal Naval College; I never saw him again. Such foolishness. Our berth at the coal wharf was unsatisfactory; it was impossible to avoid bringing wet coal dust on board, on our feet, every time we came back to AA.

The rain was almost incessant, and I remember coming on board once and going down into the aft cabin to get warm and dry, where Nigel was sitting alone, huddled over the stove. He asked me if it was always like this in November. I told him that it wouldn't last long, that we'd soon be in a warmer climate, and he'd be creeping about looking for patches of shade. He lit another cigarette and looked at me witheringly through the smoke. Nigel blamed me personally for English weather, and I felt that I owed him an ongoing apology. We eventually sailed for Falmouth on the 14th, finding a clean berth above the town towards Penryn. Here we took on some more stores and dithered while the foul weather continued unabated. It has occurred to me since that that awful late autumn of 1959 was a climatic reaction to the long hot dry summer, when week after week went by without any rain at all. At the time, however, it seemed as if it were some sort of personal affront to Nigel. Once again, as in Dartmouth, the rain pelted down and the wind whistled through the streets. I walked out to Pendennis Point one afternoon to stare at the Channel, white-capped and entirely unwelcoming. We waited a couple of days to collect some fire extinguishers and engine parts, then sailed, willy-nilly. We were so glad to leave that we didn't mind that AA rolled so heavily that she dipped her scuppers on either side; while in the galley, in spite of fiddles, the plates, mugs and pans jumped about with continual clatter.

* * * * *

It was over forty years ago, so it is hard, today, to recapture the feeling of optimism and exhilaration that I think we all felt, to be on our way. We should have been wondering what we thought we were doing, setting off across the Bay of Biscay in late November with a dismal weather forecast in an ill-equipped boat. Jim, who should have known better, was very cheerful, singing ribald songs to himself at the wheel. Dave told me about a trip he'd made to Bear Island in his trawling days, but I wasn't keen to hear about Bear Island. Our course, once we'd cleared the Lizard, lay south-southwest; we were headed for Vigo. The seas were coming at us broad on our starboard bow, which gave AA a horrible twisting motion. We had sailed on Friday the 27th. Dave didn't like sailing on a Friday. Being a trawlerman, he was riddled with superstitions, among which was the belief that sailing on a Friday was courting certain trouble. There were inauspicious words and colours too – I think green was bad, but I cannot now remember any of the words. I don't know whether today's trawlermen are similarly superstitious, but if they are, it's a wonder they ever get to sea at all. By Saturday night we were heading into a force 8 gale, and, almost unbelievably, the Monday midday weather forecast warned us of a force 12 coming our way. Force 12! This was surely unheard of – it is hurricane force. Maybe they'd made a mistake?

But I knew there was no mistake; we were in for a real pasting. The barometer started to fall (it eventually fell to 962 millibars) – I could hardly bear to look at it, while the seas coming at us from the Atlantic became more and more mountainous. There was no sun, so we could not take a sight and couldn't know precisely where we were; but we were obviously being driven east, and when the wind veered to the northwest, as it did that evening, we knew that we were fast approaching the worst of it. By this time we were running down onto the north coast of Spain; it was impossible to tell how far away that was, but I was becoming worried. Jim didn't seem to be. It occurred to me that having served entirely in large, fully powered freighters and passenger liners, he didn't have the yachtsman's fear of being set onto a lee shore. I said that I thought we should turn into the wind and try at least to stand still. I thought he might resent my encroachment on his territory – he was the navigator and had a Master's ticket. I soon learnt, when I knew Jim better, that he didn't have any vanity, self-importance or defensiveness in his make-up. We agreed, with Dave, that we should turn. By this time the wind was practically in the north, coming at us with extraordinary ferocity. The thought of turning into it was not attractive, but that is what we had to do. At half-throttle we punched our way into the great masses of Atlantic coming at us. We weren't unduly concerned – after all we were in a 70-foot North Sea trawler designed for horrible winter weather – and so long as there were no surprises for us, we could sit it out, hoping that we wouldn't get our windows broken and that nothing important would be carried away.

Jim started to sing: I think he was enjoying himself. After all, he'd seen nothing like this at sea before. Even in the worst weather he'd seen it all from the bridge, about fifty feet above sea level.

That night, November 30th, we resigned ourselves to having a very disagreeable time until the depression had passed. With Dave on the wheel I could study how well AA was coping. The sea had become yeasty, covered with great mats of foam being driven downwind, with occasional lumps being blown off the crests and coming along the deck like shrapnel. Once she was caught off balance, taking on board a large lump of water which tore the dinghy out of its lashings and hurled it along the deck, carrying away the potato peeler which was bolted to the deck. Dave said, 'There goes our potato peeler, we'll have to peel them by hand now.' I remember thinking that I would be very glad to be in harbour, peacefully peeling potatoes by hand.

The dinghy ended up jammed alongside the wheelhouse, stove in. Jim and I made a hurried sally onto the deck to secure her. Like most fishing boats of her type, AA had a gaff mizzen sail, which was set to keep her head to wind. This now began to shred, splitting along the seam in spite of the baggy-wrinkle on the stays. Our deck lights showed us these minor mishaps, but we were unprepared for the next bad thing to happen, which was that a great lump of rogue water came over the bow and lashed against the wheelhouse windows, breaking three of them and showering us with shards of glass. It cut Dave's forehead, but not seriously, so he stayed at the wheel while Jim and I took it in turns to stand with our backs to the frames, holding up oilskin coats to keep the worst weather out.

Jim had just taken over this job from me, and I had hoisted myself onto the chart table to make more room in the wheelhouse when I discovered that there was blood all over the table, and that it was covered with broken glass which had cut through my oilskin trousers into my backside. Luckily there were no charts on the table because Jim had removed the one in use and folded it small, jamming it out of harm's way in a corner. I retreated to the engine room to put some elastoplast on my bottom, where I found a grim-faced Dick. He told me that he would have to cut the engine revolutions because we had nearly run out of lubricating oil; it was burning up more quickly than we had expected. The engine was worn. We had the opportunity to buy oil in Falmouth, but it had been decided to wait until we could get it more cheaply in Vigo. Our position was starkly clear: either we maintain our revs and risk the engine seizing up when the lube oil ran out, or we cut the revs and eke it out until the weather eased. We decided to cut the revs. Also in the engine room, which was rather crowded in consequence, were Tim and Nigel. They would, no doubt, have helped me in my difficulties with the elastoplast, but they were fully engaged in trying to stop the ship's batteries from jumping out of their rack and smashing on the engine room floor. AA was pitching and rolling so violently that there was a real danger of our becoming battery-less, which would have been a major disaster.

We then entered a period when things looked desperate. With reduced power, AA's head kept falling off and so far as I could see we were making no progress at all through the water – in fact we may have been going astern. The noise of the wind changed: from a high-pitched screaming it had become what I can only describe as a sinister, loud, gloomy hum, a noise I had never heard before, have never heard since, and never wish to hear again. The ink line on the barograph was like a cliff face. I can remember feeling irritated that Dave would put the wheel over with a firm jerk at the end of its scope, an act of emphasis which I thought was unnecessary; I envisaged the servings on the spliced wire of the steering gear being chewed up in the sheaves. Jim sang all 29 verses of 'Eskimo Nell'. I was amazed that he was able to recite the whole work, without pausing or hesitation. A remarkable memory, had Jim. When he'd finished, he ignited and held up a distress flare, hanging in the mizzen shrouds by one arm and holding the flare up with the other. Tim appeared with his automatic distress machine, and he and Nigel took it in turns to wind the handle, which was hard work. Tim also tried to send a signal on the tank radio but it had been soaked and was useless. AA's head continued to keep falling off, first one side then the other. At one point, Pam had a piece of bad luck in that she chose to open the hatch from the galley into the wheelhouse at the very moment when another wave broke aboard. A large part of it came through the broken windows at us, continuing unchecked into the galley, right in her face. She disappeared and shut the hatch, spluttering. So we continued, through the night. At intervals I peered astern, dreading to see the iron-bound coast of Galicia, but could discern nothing through the blackness.

Very early in the morning we saw a most welcome sight. A large trawler, or possibly a small coaster, appeared about one hundred yards away on our starboard side, with deck lights on and scrambling nets over the side. We could see that the crew were gesturing at us to use the nets. I measured the distance by eye, took off my short sea boots preparing for a swim, hoping it wouldn't be necessary. She stayed there for about two hours, then, concluding that we could manage after all, sheered away and disappeared. We never knew who she was, but were very grateful to her for standing by us – it had been a lonely vigil.

Dawn came, December 1st, and the wind dropped to a gale force 7/8, which seemed like a calm after what had gone before. We stared at each other in that ghastly dawn, the wind dropped more, the barograph kicked up, and we shaped a course for Corunna. We could see the Spanish coast by this time, most inhospitable, about five miles away, and were able to establish our position at about forty miles to the east of Corunna. Our engine continued to turn over in a languid, peaceful way, as if it had all the time in the world, while AA threw herself around all over the place, plunging, staggering and crashing in the aftermath of the storm, tossed by a sea for which the word 'confused' would be inadequate. Demented would be better. We crept along the coast like a whipped dog, round Cape Ortegal, into Corunna harbour, tying up in the fish dock in the late afternoon. Nigel described, in a letter to his wife, how we appeared – 'the wheelhouse in a shambles, and rope and chains scattered about the deck like grandma's knitting'. I climbed up onto the dockside but found that I couldn't stand – the ground under my feet seemed to leap and roll in the oddest way – so I went back on board to lie down in one of the bunks in the aft cabin, hoping someone would light the stove. I felt both tired and very excited. I couldn't sleep, but lay there with images of the past two days whirling round in my mind. I suppose, although it didn't occur to me at the time, I had been pumping adrenalin.

We all admired AA. We could hardly have believed the power and seeming malevolence of that wind, but she had coped magnificently, hurled about, thumped unmercifully. Now she lay motionless in the oily scum of the fishing harbour. She seemed smug, as if saying, 'Next time, make sure that you've got enough lube oil.' That indeed is a lesson we had learned. She had acquired, during the storm, a personality which we all admired and respected; I felt that she knew her job better than we did ours. Jim said, 'By the time we get to Auckland, we'll love every inch of her.'

It may well be asked, What was Skipper Les doing all this time? He was stretched on his bunk, prostrate with seasickness, which makes it all the more amazing that he had ever wanted to embark on this adventure in the first place. People are very odd; yet, as will become apparent, we needed him, and certain qualities which he alone possessed, on several occasions during the passage. The hurricane had, in a sense, sorted us out. There was no doubt that Jim was the essential member of the crew: so far as we had a captain, it was he. His only weakness was in areas where he had no experience, and they were few. The Merchant Navy no longer had time to teach cadets about sailing so he knew nothing about it, but he became very interested in it as time went by. He was, I think, a natural seaman, a square peg in a square hole. Both he and Dave were utterly imperturbable; I did the worrying for both of them.

We now had every confidence in AA, but she was a shambles. Nigel described her in a letter: 'She looked a mess next morning, sail in shreds and broken rigging hanging down, doors off the main hatch, dinghy smashed.' The effect on the crew was rather more submerged. For my part, the immediate result was a great desire for sweets – presumably to replace sugar. I remember going to the cinema to see a new version of *The Four Feathers*, dubbed into Spanish, and eating a whole box of Meltis Fruits. Keith was our only complete casualty. He started to behave oddly, to the point where Les felt obliged to book him into a nursing home in the town. Shortly after that he went home, and Nigel wrote to a friend, John, asking him if he'd like to join. Whether this was a very friendly thing to do, and whether Nigel told John what to expect, I'm not sure; but, nothing daunted, John joined us soon afterward. He was another Australian, by adoption, but not by birth, so not as Australian as Nigel himself. There are, I had discovered, degrees of Australian-ness; it would be a major undertaking to analyse this phenomenon. John joined as an engineer but he was versatile; eventually he demonstrated that he could catch fish better than anyone else on board, although this was disputed at the time.

We soon discovered that 'our' hurricane had not been an isolated incident, nor was it the end of the matter. As that awful first week of December 1959 unfolded, I could follow the tragic story in *The Times* each day. While we were enduring our difficulties off the north coast of Spain, the Union Castle liner *Braemar Castle* (17,000 tons) went aground in a southwesterly gale at Punta Mala, between Gibraltar and Algeciras, and soon after, *Oronsay* (27,000 tons) and *Chusan* (24,000 tons) had to shelter at Algeciras having been unable to dock in Gibraltar. Seventy mph cyclonic winds swept Lisbon, while a fishing boat with all seven of her crew was lost off Viana do Castelo. The national rowing champion was drowned when his dinghy capsized on the River Minho. Torrents of rain swept Spain, disrupting communications in the north and centre. It was the same on the Riviera – the railway from Nice to Ventimiglia was cut, and the Nice–Cagnes road closed. The sea came into the centre of Nice, with three-foot waves breaking over the Promenade des Anglais. Snow followed in Spain – heavy falls in the north, floods in Zamora. Under pressure from the swollen waters of the River Reyran the Malpasset dam burst, drowning 270 people in Frejus in Var, in the south of France. Italy didn't escape: there was a landslide in the Aosta valley and the Po and Ticino rivers overflowed. In Genoa there was 'one of the most violent sea storms of recent years' with serious damage to Pegli, Voltri, Savona and Charavi, plus snow in Turin. Later in that first week of December a Portuguese ocean-going tug was lost off Oporto and her seventeen crew all drowned, while the Scottish fishing vessel *George Robb* was lost when she was driven onto rocks off Dunscanby Head. All her twelve crew were drowned. The dredger *Port Sunlight* went down off Flamborough Head with two crew drowned, and the lifeboat *Mona* was driven ashore near Carnoustie. The Broughty Ferry lifeboat was lost with eight crew drowned. On December 10th the crew of seven from the North Carr lightship had to be rescued, but that at last brought to an end the disasters of 1959.

All of this I gleaned from *The Times* while we lay snug in Corunna harbour; I think now that it is from our own experience on the night of November 30th and from reading about this string of tragedies that I can date a fear of the sea and what it can do. We had been swiped by the hurricane and got away with it – on that occasion. We had been foolish: setting off without sufficient lubricating oil for a worn engine, hardly deserving to escape when so many well-prepared craft had been stricken.

One of the first things we did after arrival was to have a celebratory dinner at the Embajador Hotel. It was the only occasion when we all dressed formally, so far as we were able, and it was a great success. The hotel gave us a splendid meal, we drank a lot, while the evening was only slightly marred by another dinner going on in the next room attended by an unnerving group of army officers with a sprinkling of priests, a quiet and portentous gathering reflecting Franco's Spain in one of its more unattractive aspects. Looking through the dividing doors at this jowly group of power brokers, I felt that I was seeing a sample of the Caudillo's establishment, and it was not reassuring. No doubt if the Communists had been the winners, the group would have been much the same in physiognomy, but in different clothes.

We didn't know then that we would be in Corunna for more than two months, although we should have guessed that nothing would happen quickly. The insurers had to agree every repair, and every repair involved delay. Les's negotiating skills were deployed to good effect during this period. Our dinghy was repaired and all storm damage made good, with the exception of the shredded sail. The potato peeler was not replaced, but no doubt a payment for it was made and diverted to some other more pressing need. Then AA was slipped for an examination of her bottom, although I failed to see – still fail to see – what possible claim could be made for any underwater damage. Her propeller was removed and put back again, on general principles, and from my point of view this was a welcome opportunity to have a look at her underwater shape. I was agreeably surprised to see that she did not have a bad sailing hull at all, with fairly fine lines, promising that she could be driven through the water with a small sail area, given good conditions. I had already guessed that she would move quite well, because under power, when I looked over her stern, there was little disturbance in the water; she didn't drag half the sea behind her.

All this caused me to cheer up and become more optimistic about our ocean crossings. I set about repairing the battered mizzen. George helped me, but insisted that sail repair could only be carried out under good weather conditions. 'You have to have the sun on your back,' he said. That didn't happen very often. Corunna was very wet that winter – perhaps it always is – so our sail repairs were infrequent and erratic, but with two months at our disposal we did in fact complete the job on the mizzen, sewing the bolt-rope back onto it and restitching the seams. When we had finished, it was serviceable, but I could see that it would not stand up to hard service because the canvas was too chafed. Fortunately, we had another mizzen, which was promoted to being *the* mizzen, while the damaged one was designated to be mizzen topsail; but that is to anticipate our final dispositions to be made in the Canary Islands.

Les, Pam, and to a lesser extent I, spent time with the British consul in Corunna, who was very helpful. He became a good friend to Les and on several occasions he drove us around the country in his car, sampling the local wines in various inns. I am bound to say that I found these to be uniformly awful, forming the opinion that Galicia is not a natural wine-growing area. On one dreadful occasion we visited a pub where the proud proprietor lined up a succession of wines on the counter for us to sample – about eight in a row. To refuse would have been out of the question, but each was more horrid than the last. Les didn't seem to mind, Pam was excused, but my stomach rebelled later so I avoided future expeditions. Our social centre ashore, our club, was the Astoria Bar in the town, and as the weeks went by we became accustomed to the life of Corunna. Every morning I would see the lottery ticket seller outside the bread shop, while one of the more familiar sights was a young army officer, a pearl-handled revolver on his hip, who could be seen promenading with a different girl on his arm on each occasion. He seemed to have no military duties.

At Christmas, the citizens put on their best clothes, paraded with their children, the bells in all the churches jangled, and the town was *en fête*. One bitterly cold day, Dick, Dave and I took a bus to Santiago de Compostela. It left at about 5:30 a.m., so part of the journey was in the dark, through a stony poor-seeming landscape. Travelling in the comparative luxury of our bus, looking out at the bleak stony landscape of Galicia, I thought of the desperate British army which, exactly 151 years before, had straggled along a road a little to the east of the one we were taking; harried by Napoleon's dragoons, frozen, starving, demoralised and taking no notice of their officers. The retreat to Corunna was one of those events in British army history which are regarded as being some sort of triumph, like Dunkirk, but which was undeniably a defeat. Napoleon's army, under Soult, was checked at the final battle outside Corunna, so I suppose that could be called a tactical success; but as the entire army was embarked immediately afterwards, it was a peculiarly British sort of victory. The general in command, Sir John Moore, was extremely able. He had had to choose between Vigo and Corunna as the place of embarkation for his heavily outnumbered army. He chose Corunna because his engineers reported that it was the more defensible town to protect an embarkation, so the transports were therefore ordered to gather there. The retreat to Corunna displayed the characteristics of a British–Irish army very clearly. It was said that our army in retreat can be gleaned but not reaped. Although discipline collapsed in large part while retreating (not, it should be added, among the Guards) nevertheless when the worn-out wretches turned to fight, it was with amazing ferocity and success. Another odd quirk displayed by these men was that when the French general

Colbert was killed in a cavalry attack, the historian Napier tells us, 'His fine martial figure, his voice, his gestures, and, above all, his daring valour had excited the admiration of the British, and a general feeling of sorrow was predominant when the gallant soldier fell.'

It never really became light that day – it must have been early January – and the most notable memory I retain of the outing was the amazing sight of the façade of the great cathedral, with falling snow slanting across it. After our breakfast we walked through the huge building, shivering, peering at the ornate silver decorated chapels. It was a strange experience, at the dead of the year, under the very worst conditions, to see this great place of pilgrimage. We took a train back in the middle of the morning. Third class had wooden seats and a large number of women taking hens to market in wicker cages. The train was very slow and fitted with square wheels. On arrival in Corunna station I was dismayed to find, in the public lavatory, 'Kilroy was here' scrawled on the wall. It seemed inappropriate, I'm not sure why.

I appreciated the Corunna dogs, of which there were many, good-natured and noisy. The Spanish seemed indulgent to dogs, who were given great license. Our sleep was often disturbed by their continual barking. There was one very dirty dog who came into harbour on top of a pile of timber in a small boat from Corcubion which moored alongside us. Someone threw a warp, inadvertently striking this animal, who barked in consequence for about half an hour. Then there was a large team of dogs who were permanently encamped on a pile of timber on the dockside, supposedly engaged in ratting although I never saw them working. They reminded me of a group of soldiers in a railway station, taking their ease on their kit bags, waiting for a train. Nigel was very interested in these animals, wanting to train them and bring them into some sort of order, which included giving them all a bath. I told him that he would be wasting his time – but it would be nice if we could have baths ourselves, never mind the dogs.

One of my most vivid and abiding memories of Corunna was of a great event which took place at regular, but wide, intervals; very moving, which I am glad I did not miss. The liner *Begonia* would depart for South America with emigrants on board. I witnessed this twice during our stay, and it carried all the emotional weight of long family separation. I don't know where *Begonia* was going – Caracas? Barranquilla? – but she certainly left in style. Bands played, streamers fluttered between ship and shore, families waved, shouted, wept, lamenting and contorting themselves. Fortunately the band didn't play 'Auld Lang Syne' – that would have been unbearable – but perhaps they rendered the Spanish equivalent.

We spent Christmas on the slips, much to Muriel's annoyance because it meant a long climb up and down a ladder to leave the boat. In spite of this we ate a fine Christmas dinner 'with all the trimmings', drinking some Carlos IV brandy, which was one of the better brands. I cannot remember now in what order of quality the various Carlos brandies progressed – whether the worst was Carlos I, getting better as you went up the scale, or whether it was the other way round. There were some formidably bad brandies available, by French standards. I remember Terry and Fundador as being popular, but it was usual to put a match to the surface before drinking in order to get rid of the methylated spirit flavour.

By New Year's Eve we were back afloat, our New Year's celebrations involving another good meal and a great deal of hooting from all the craft in the harbour. The most impressive was a great sonorous blast from a big ore freighter at the other side of the port: our own little hoarse squeak was contemptible.

I had meant, while in the town – although we had not originally intended to call – to visit the memorial to Sir

John Moore. Looking out over Corunna harbour, it was still possible to imagine the rescue fleet – 250-strong, including store ships, transports and warships – waiting to rescue the battered and exhausted army. There is something greatly appealing about Moore, one of – I nearly wrote 'England's', but then remembered he was a Scot – Britain's most attractive soldiers, and a great trainer of men. Colonel Napier describes him in his dignified post-Gibbonian prose as 'a man whose uncommon capacity was sustained by the purest virtue, and governed by a disinterested patriotism more in keeping with the primitive than the luxurious age of a great nation. His tall graceful person, his dark searching eyes, strongly defined forehead, and singularly expressive mouth, indicated a noble disposition and a refined understanding. The lofty sentiments of honour habitual to his mind, adorned by a subtle playful wit, gave him in conversation an ascendancy that he could well preserve by the decisive vigour of his actions.' Napier sustains this level of writing for over 3000 pages, throughout six volumes; I wonder how many colonels could match him today? However, I did not visit his memorial, partly because I didn't know where to look and was too idle to find out, and partly because it was cold and wet. But I regretted this later. Apparently the memorial was erected by the French, which was a generous gesture.

* * * * *

At long last, on February 7th we sailed, all bills paid and the last repair completed. We had had one stroke of remarkably good luck during the last weeks of our stay. Lying alongside us for a short period was a small German freighter and, as was his wont, Les became friendly with the captain and the chief engineer. There was a good deal of drinking and camaraderie over two or three days before Tim told me that the chief engineer, with the agreement of his captain, was going to fill up our diesel tank for nothing. Apparently, the ship could spare a few tons of fuel without noticing it: in our case, four tons. This amazed me. I thought ships' owners kept a tight control on such matters – they certainly used to – but we were all delighted. The chief engineer had served aboard U-boats during the war, being one of the few survivors of a peculiarly ill-fated branch of the German Navy. For some reason which I cannot explain, this had made him fond of British seagoing people, therefore well-disposed towards us and anxious to help. Perhaps he had been plucked out of the sea by the Royal Navy – who knows? – but whatever the reason, it was his idea that we should be treated to the free fuel. The transaction took place at night, because neither we nor the Germans wanted the Spanish police to notice what was going on; I'm not sure why, but no doubt they would have found something irregular about it which would have involved us in trouble or expense. So, in the dead of night, a hose was passed from our friendly neighbour over our deck to our tanks, and the diesel pumped in. We sailed soon after this, with full tanks. I cannot say that we left Corunna with any regret; we had been there too long and were all aching to get away. To be at sea again was a delight, as we rolled along at about five knots towards Cape Villano.

We had just rounded the Cape and had altered course to take us down the coast to Vigo, when our engine stopped. It was not clear to me exactly what had gone wrong but it seemed to involve the failure of the water pump: the engineers didn't tell us all that went on in the engine room. We wallowed in a light breeze, with Cape Villano a mile or so to port. Luckily the wind was from the northeast, and the tide was setting us down the coast in the direction we wanted to go, but something had to be done to give us steerage way. I pulled out *Gratitude*'s big jib from under Jim's bunk and hoisted it on the forestay. It pulled beautifully and gave us about two knots – enough to answer the helm properly. Jim was impressed. 'At a time like this,' he said generously, 'I might as well tear up my ticket and throw it over the side.'

We weren't entirely alone: a German schooner, under power and sail, circled round us a couple of times to make sure we weren't in serious trouble, then sheered off. It was very quiet and peaceful, the silence broken only by the clink of tools and an occasional expletive from the engine room. We had a cup of tea. And so we went on into the night, until, at about 3:00 a.m., the engine started again. It was decided that we should go into Vigo, as our trouble, whatever it was, needed the attention of a marine engineer. On reflection, it is strange that we were not more perturbed by this incident. After all, we had been very lucky, with all conditions in our favour, but it might so easily have been otherwise. Perhaps we had become fatalistic, or inured to mishap – I don't know – but thinking back to my own attitude at the time, I can only recall my satisfaction that the jib was doing so well. I also think that we had confidence in our engineers; they would fix it, no doubt about it.

We tied up in the Vigo fish dock on February 8th, and Dick, with Tim to help with translation and general support, went to find an engineer. Apparently what happened, as Tim told me later, is that the Spanish engineer said yes, he could repair the pump, and it would cost about the equivalent of £35. Tim went through a performance of being appalled and downcast, telling the Spaniard that we weren't yachtsmen (I would have thought that was obvious) and couldn't possibly afford such a huge sum. The Spaniard asked what it would cost in England. Tim said 'about £17', so the Spaniard agreed to that amount. We were becoming quite experienced at this sort of show.

It rained solidly for the 36 hours we lay in Vigo. I found a bookshop which sold English books, a shelf of them in a dark corner, many of which had probably been there for years. I bought an Everyman copy of *Dr. Thorne*, Pascal's *Pensées*, also *The Year of the Dog* by Don Byrne, Rose Macaulay's *Fabled Shore*, and *The Mill on the Floss*. I was delighted with my find – I hadn't expected such success. The long stay in Corunna had used up most of our reading matter; paperbacks tended to disintegrate after they had passed through a few hands and of course the most popular disappeared first. *Dr. Thorne* was a surprising success. Jim read it, going about saying 'Sir Omicron Pie' to himself and chuckling, but that was much later.

Having quickly exhausted the delights of Vigo we sailed for Lisbon, moving down the coast in a tossy force 6 from the west northwest. As we approached the Tagus, I studied through my binoculars a huge building lying back from the coast which I assumed to be the great monastery of Mafra, whose vast echoing galleries I had visited ten years before. It was good to be seeing Portugal again. We rounded into the Tagus, and were directed to lie in the Alcantara dock. This was a scene of extreme confusion, full of a wide variety of craft. It was a Saturday so many of the boats had come to dock for the weekend. We had to take our luck with the rest and at one point we found ourselves under the stern of a Norwegian freighter whose stern warp tightened against our mizzen backstay in a threatening way. For a few seconds it looked as if we were going to lose our precious mizzen – it jerked and jumped in its tabernacle as our backstay took the strain of the freighter's great manilla warp which was rubbing across it like a huge bow on a violin string. The warp was visibly chafing away in front of our eyes, with bits flying off it, while a couple of sailors were lounging over the stern watching with complete unconcern. We shouted: 'Slack your stern warp!', but they just smiled. Jim was furious – 'Bloody useless Scowegians' – and if Dave could have reached up to thump them, he would. One would have thought that even though they weren't bothered about our mizzen, they might have minded about their stern warp, but no. Just before disaster, the warp slacked with no more damage than the loss of our ensign staff, which snapped off, and we edged clear.

We eventually found a mooring at a buoy, where an official came aboard to decide our final disposition. He and Les had a long conversation in the wheelhouse, after which Les came to tell me that we were on the horns of a dilemma. If we were to be classified as a yacht, we would have to prove our status and this is where my help was needed. I was a member of the Cruising Association, and had a yachting cap with the CA badge on the front. Would I therefore put on the cap and provide evidence of membership? I had my membership card, so I showed it and put on the cap. So: we were a yacht. But not so fast, Mr Captain – if we were a yacht then we must, in the commercial harbour, have a policeman on board for the period of our visit. It so happened that there was a policeman handy for the job right there, a great grim-faced thug, whom we would have to feed and accommodate. Dr Salazar, who had been running Portugal for decades, and who had a legal/academic background, had had plenty of time to fine-tune all the state systems. Les and I had a quick discussion – better pay the charges, we decided, after another look at the alternative, who was glowering at us from the aft deck. But Les thought it would be worth having a little more argument with the official. I don't know what he said – I moved away in order not to cramp his style – but after another ten minutes of talk, both the official and the policeman went away and we neither paid the larger harbour dues nor accommodated the latter. Quite what sort of Great Australian bite Les had put on the official I don't know. We all tended to leave him alone with his victims while we drifted away embarrassed but admiring.

I have always liked Portugal, with its strange Manueline architecture and colourful azulejos tiles. It seems to me that they are all of a piece with the people. It couldn't have been much fun living under Salazar all those years, yet they seemed very cheerful. Bill and I paid a visit to the tower of Belem, leaning on the parapet overlooking the Tagus, in the warm sunshine. It seemed a quirky and frivolous fort, but was apparently built in all earnestness to protect the entrance of the river, a delightful fun building as it appeared. George, Muriel and I made an expedition to Sintra by train; I had visited in 1949 and had found it to be the most attractive of all the Portuguese towns. On the train, sitting opposite us between a middle-aged couple, was a cosseted smooth-haired black and white dog of indeterminate breed. He was very clean and pampered looking, with a red ribbon in his collar, sitting between his owners quietly, staring at us as if weighing up the possibility of titbits being offered. A calculating animal, but good-natured and well-behaved. Occasionally one of his owners would address a word to him in Portuguese, but he continued staring hopefully.

Sintra was much as I had remembered it from my visit ten years earlier, but on this occasion it happened to be market day, which proved a great bonus. We were amazed at the variety of goods on display – monkeys, old swords in bundles, engravings and watercolours, clothes, walking sticks, basket work, birds in cages, the *Encyclopaedia Britannica*, volumes of Charles Dickens' works, pottery, glass, and of course a great array of food. Muriel wanted to buy all sorts of things, mostly of a domestic nature, but was restrained by George who reminded her that we had a long way to go yet and shouldn't spend too much in the Sintra market. I bought a copy of *Bleak House*, which I had never read, thinking that it would occupy a few idle hours on the long passages ahead. Sintra was delightful, very lush, green and mild. We sat in the town square drinking, watching the passing scene. We decided that we wouldn't, after all, go up to the Pena Palace. I had seen it in 1949 and had been amazed by it, although it is not recommended by the Michelin Guide which doesn't give it even a single star. It is a Scottish baronial type palace, built by Fernando II in the 1840s. Fernando was cousin to our own Prince Consort Albert, and they seem to have shared the same architectural tastes. Sitting in the balmy sunshine in Sintra square, AA with all her past and coming difficulties seemed far away.

On our return to Lisbon, we were soon reminded of more down-to-earth and pressing concerns. A huge 98 lb Calor gas bottle was delivered on board, to be manhandled into the WC compartment and connected up to the galley gas piping. We didn't buy any diesel fuel. It was not a place where it could be bought cheaply; in any case, after our windfall in Corunna, we hardly had need of any yet. The plan was to fill up the tanks in the Canary Islands, preparatory to the Atlantic crossing. I hoped that we would be able to sail at least half the way from Tenerife to Barbados, but with a consumption of 85 gallons per day under power, under favourable conditions, we thought it would be at least prudent to start with full tanks. George thought that it would be a good idea to look for a German freighter to get alongside, but this was not felt to be a serious suggestion.

We stayed in Lisbon for a week, leaving on February 20th, and ran into a force 7 immediately we had left the Tagus, from the southwest, accompanied by heavy rain and poor visibility. Jim and I were still working our six-on, six-off routine, and it fell to me to be on watch when we entered the Straits of Gibraltar. Suddenly ships were coming at us from all directions, in the dark. Huge tankers pounded up astern in the most threatening manner, overtaking us on either side, and I had a mental picture of the officers of the watch, with their feet up in the chart room, laughing at us on their radar screens. I had never been so glad to see Jim as when he came on watch at dawn.

We tied up in Gibraltar harbour in the middle of the

morning, close by a Sailors' Canteen where good Norwegian beer was sold, to stay there for five days. Bill and I went for a long walk up the side of the rock by zigzag paths, encountering the ubiquitous apes, one of whom climbed onto Bill's shoulders and pulled his ears. I took a photograph of this episode, which I was told is typical. Les, Pam and I took a gharry ride around the town, looking at the shops but not buying anything. Later Bill and I took the ferry to Algeciras for a couple of hours, so that we could say we had seen the town, although it was not attractive. There was a large quantity of mail waiting for us at the harbour office, and for me there was a consignment of two large tins of assorted sweet biscuits which arrived in a van with Carr's Biscuits painted on the front, which my mother had sent from Carlisle. These biscuits were not immediately broached, but were to be the basis of the tea parties which became a feature of our Atlantic crossing. One morning, I was walking through the town and came to the Governor's palace, where a parade was taking place outside the front entrance. A band played, soldiers marched, sergeants shouted words of command; all was carried out with great precision, and I felt that here there was still a shred of Empire. I thought of that poem by Wilfred Scawen Blunt, *Gibraltar*. I couldn't remember how it went, but have looked it up since and it fitted the occasion perfectly, so well in fact, that Blunt must have witnessed a similar ceremony:

> *At this door*
> *England stands sentry. God! To hear the shrill*
> *Sweet treble of her fifes upon the breeze,*
> *And at the summons of the rock gun's roar*
> *To see her redcoats marching from the hill!*

Such thoughts were not altogether acceptable, even in 1960, at a time when we were preparing to leave most of Africa and had long left India, so I didn't mention them to anyone except George who, as an old Navy man, had some old-fashioned views.

While we were in Gibraltar we took the opportunity to freshen up the interior of AA. She had become, let's face it, dank and foetid. Rain had fallen on us for much of the time since leaving Southwick, and now at last we seemed to be in a period of warm sunshine. All bedding was hauled up from below and festooned on deck to air. The fo'c'sle that Jim and I occupied was fortunate in having a large square hatch which could be left open, but the aft cabin was rather more difficult to sweeten. A determined effort was made to 'clear up', everybody wanting to throw away other people's unwanted gear. Tim was accused of spreading his property like a weed growing along shelves that didn't strictly belong to his bunk space. There was no problem with the centre cabins where the women ruled. I made an attempt – or rather Pam made an attempt, with my help – to reorganise the food compartment. This had to be done with the aid of a torch, and some sort of order was established among the tins, the rice, corn flakes, porridge oats, pineapple chunks, etc. Jim examined his charts, and Dick did obscure things in the engine room.

When we sailed, on February 27th, to make the short passage to Tangier, a fresh Levanter was blowing out of the straits, so I decided to try out the twin boomed staysails. They pulled well, but the wind stream was broken by the wheelhouse so that the boom of each sail lifted alternately, spilling the wind and reducing the effect. I thought it would be a good idea, when we reached Tenerife, to fit kicking straps to pin down the booms. We didn't stop the engine while I was carrying out this test, and we made good progress through a bright green sea. Muriel put her head out of the galley scuttle to complain that 'playing about with the sails' was making things even more difficult in there than they normally were. Not everybody thought it was fun to sail rather than motor.

When we reached Tangier, Les's tongue was once more called into service. We found that we had given offence by not flying the flag of Morocco as a courtesy when we entered the harbour. I don't think that when Les had been purchasing the flags we had planned to call at Tangier, but whatever the reason, the harbour official was not pleased. Les explained (and on this occasion I happened to hear the exchange) that we were an impecunious bunch and had economised on flags, we were very sorry indeed, but hoped that a well-known port like Tangier wouldn't care much if a ratbag ship like AA omitted the normal courtesy. All of that went down quite well; the official did not make an issue of the flag, but reminded Les that just because we were a British boat did not mean that we could behave in a typically insolent British way. Les said that indeed the British were inclined to be supercilious and neglectful of other nations' rights, which he, as an Australian, had often found offensive. The official was mollified: you had to hand it to Les. After that exchange, we could not complain about our berth in the harbour, a long walk from the town at a quayside where the Levanter whisked dust and rubbish onto our decks. My memories of Tangier in Ramadan are dominated by waking at night to the sound of the Muezzin's call to prayer echoing round the city from the loudspeakers on the minarets. To lie snug in my berth and hear this incomprehensible but mesmeric sound, drifting in and out of sleep, was blissful, like a delightful dream. Bill and I explored the kasbah, which was in marked contrast to the modern European-designed part of the town. Bill saw some spilt blood which he insisted was the result of a knife fight but which I thought had probably been the scene of a goat's despatch. Bill liked drama.

There was no need for us to stay in Tangier so we sailed on March 1st, with the satisfactory sense that we were 'getting on'. We plodded easily down the Moroccan coast in warm sunshine, making about five knots. We were beginning to enjoy ourselves. I had a long conversation with Jim, sitting up forward in the eyes of the ship and watching the tawny, arid coast slip by. He told me about his life at sea, on the Indian coast and in the South China Sea where, he told me, he had seen some dreadful weather, but nothing to equal 'our' hurricane. He reminisced about Japan and some of the Conradian places he had visited in the Far East. I told him about the realities of yacht broking, about which he had the strangest ideas. He had told me that he would rather have my life, 'sipping pink gins in my Tuxedo on the aft decks of luxury yachts', than any number of sea adventures. He didn't like any romantic ideas about seafaring to be expressed, and in particular he disputed that there had been any pleasure in handling the sailing ships of the nineteenth century. He reckoned that the owners had skimped on food, equipment and, perhaps most dangerously, on the number of crew in order to maximise profit in a tough market. He thought that there was no glamour in life at sea. I asked him what he thought he was doing on the *Aberdeen Anzac*, but he just smiled enigmatically. In Jim I felt I was hearing the authentic voice of the seagoing professional, but in spite of himself he had been unable to resist taking part in our quixotic project. That evening, as the light faded on a tranquil night, I had a sense of Africa looming, huge and forbidding on our port side: what Conrad would almost certainly have described as an 'immensity' – and he probably would also have worked in an 'unspeakable' somewhere.

On our third night out from Tangier I was on watch in the wheelhouse at about 1:00 a.m. when I noticed a remarkable phenomenon. It was a night of full moon, and round the moon itself I saw a bright halo at about the width of an outstretched hand in distance from it. As I had never seen anything like it before I handed over the wheel to the engineer who was in the wheelhouse with me – I think it was Dick – and went to get my copy of *Meteorology for Seamen,* on which I depended for all matters of weather. It told me that a ring round the moon indicated some great eruption or natural disturbance throwing up huge quantities of dust into the stratosphere, from which the moon's light was reflected. I threw the book onto the chart table, thinking it had let me down badly and that I would have to get a more reliable informant. We speculated on the real cause, guessing that we were doomed to suffer some more disagreeable weather. Tim told me at breakfast time that there had been an earthquake at Agadir, which lay about 100 miles to the southeast. He had known about this earlier but had not told us, thinking that we had enough to worry about: 'I didn't want to panic you,' he said. The radio news had been in French so he had only been able to gather the gist of what had happened, but as the reports unfolded in greater detail over the next few days we realised how great a disaster it had been. The following night, rushing past us just before dawn, the rescue fleet headed for the stricken city. Agadir had been largely destroyed and by March 5th it had been announced that there were over 10,000 dead. A great tidal wave had passed under us, completely unnoticed, and we learned that the eruption had taken place at the very time that we had been leaving Tangier. I had an uneasy feeling that we were being attended by natural disasters as we travelled and that we would eventually be overwhelmed.

Soon we sighted Fuertaventura to the west, a barren, desert-like island where we had no intention of stopping, then altered course for Las Palmas in Grand Canary. I was on watch when we arrived off the entrance to the harbour. Although possibly Jim would have taken her in, I didn't have his confidence, or indeed his sharp eyesight, so we sat about outside from about 3:00 a.m. until it was light enough to see what we were doing. It was a most tiresome and dreary three hours for me and Nigel, who was with me in the wheelhouse, bouncing up and down in a seaway on reciprocal courses, backwards and forwards at a distance of about two miles from the harbour entrance. We talked about my plans for making AA sail, agreeing that we'd find a timber merchant and select a suitable spar to carry the big jib to the best advantage, which he could then fashion to his own high standard.

I don't know what I had expected of Las Palmas, but the reality was disappointing – a matter of cranes, sheds and oil tanks. Nigel wrote to his wife: 'So far I am not greatly impressed with Las Palmas. This island anyway is very barren looking with rugged ranges reaching to 6000 feet. The town sprawls along the foreshore and then spreads in rather disordered fashion up the hillsides.' We didn't stay long, just long enough to buy some fruit and pick up our mails, then sailed for Santa Cruz in Tenerife, on March 8th. Santa Cruz was much more to our liking, a delightful place with a temperature seemingly hovering around 70 degrees, full of hibiscus and bougainvillea.

The first consideration, for me at any rate, was to create an effective sailing rig to get us across the Atlantic. I knew that the twin headsails were effective: the only modification necessary to them was to fit kicking straps to the booms to stop them spilling the wind as they lifted into the air. This we did, and they were no further trouble with the exception of a mishap in the Pacific months later when a sudden squall broke one of the booms. There were still a few remaining attentions needed to our sails. I had had sailmakers' needles sent out by the Cruising Association, who were very quick and efficient; we already had a couple of palms, so George and I sat there like two old tars, observing the passing Tenerife scene. George shared some of his naval reminiscences with me, including some hair-raising tales of events aboard destroyers during the war. We had another mizzen, which was supposed to be the reserve, but which I soon realised had become our best. This replaced the repaired one, which in turn became a mizzen topsail and hung upside down over its replacement. There was yet another very frail sail which I intended should be set between the masts when conditions served, but which certainly wouldn't survive anything much more than a force 4. *Gratitude*'s big jib was dragged out again and pressed into service as – well, I don't really know what: a sort of bastard mizzen staysail I suppose.

Nigel and I went to the timber yard, as planned, to find a suitable piece of wood, and here I should introduce our friend Rastus. Shortly after we arrived in Santa Cruz we had been befriended by an Abyssinian whose real name was Ralph Thompson, but we always knew him as Rastus. He made sure that we weren't swindled in any of our undertakings. A large cheerful man who always wore a pale lemon-coloured suit and a tie, he was invaluable to us. It was not very clear what he was doing in Santa Cruz and we could never see what he gained by giving us so much of his time. He could easily see that we had very little money, and I can only assume that he was a genuinely disinterested friend. He nearly persuaded me to give up smoking, pointing out how much I would be able to buy with the money I saved. With Rastus we went to the timber yard to get the wood which Nigel then fashioned into a boom to spread the jib. On one end of it he fitted an iron ring with a spike which fitted into the mizzen shroud thimble, on the starboard side, about ten feet above deck level. The sail itself was about 27 feet long in the luff and when hoisted it filled the whole space between deck and masthead. It was crude but effective – worked out from first principles. I believe Nigel was pleased with his handiwork. I say 'believe' because he was not one to make much display of satisfaction nor was he ever, to my knowledge, guilty of enthusiasm. Sometimes I would catch his eye and detect what I can only call a glint of wary humour.

I was particularly interested to see Tenerife because of a book, *Teneriffe and Grand Canary*, which my great-grandfather, Isaac Latimer, had written and published in 1887. I hadn't brought it with me; it was – is – elegantly bound and would have suffered, as did all our books, from damp and general attrition. In the 1880s the Canary Islands were being promoted in Britain as a delightful holiday resort, and I imagine that there was some pecuniary advantage to him arising from the lavish praise he heaped on the hotels, steamship companies, climate and in fact practically everything to do with the islands. Written in a slightly Pooterish and orotund style – typical of the time – he told his readers all they could possibly want to know, and certainly more than they needed to know about the ship he sailed in, the islands, the people, the flora, the price of everything; all buttressed by a mass of statistics. All this was published first in his newspaper, the *Western Daily Mercury* of Plymouth, and then in book form because 'the writer has been repeatedly asked to re-issue them in a more permanent form'.

Isaac was a remarkably spry old fellow of 73 when he embarked with his daughter Selena on the SS *Arawa* of the Shaw, Savill and Albion Line on February 26th, 1887. *Arawa* ran on the regular New Zealand service, calling at Santa Cruz four to five days out from Plymouth. As soon as he was on board, Isaac started running about, energetic and almost incredibly nosy. He greatly admired *Arawa*. She moved 'so noiselessly that we could hardly recognise any action in the ship at all. There was none of that puffing and blowing which so disturbs the feelings of the passengers of many steamers, and as this silence continued to pervade the ship throughout our stay in it, I may as well state that it arises from the new triple-expansion system of engines with which the *Arawa* and her sister ship, the *Tanui*, were fitted.' He made a special visit to the quarters of the 'third class single men passengers', pointing out to his readers that 'It is a great object on these ships to keep the unmarried people separate.' I wonder. They were emigrants, and when he visited them 'they were at blanket drill ... most of the blankets were already folded and in their places on the berths, looking the picture of soldierly order.'

I wonder what he would have thought of *Aberdeen Anzac*. He was particularly interested in New Zealand, having been, in his youth, appointed an agent for emigration to the new colony, and in great enthusiasm he had, as a young reporter on the *West Briton* of Truro, given a lecture to the Truro Society in 1843, dressed up as a Maori warrior, in feathers, and carrying some sort of knobkerry, on life in New Zealand. This was, I suppose, intended to encourage emigration to the new colony, although it seems to me to have been an odd sort of encouragement. He never went to New Zealand himself, but one of his nephews went, the son of his brother Tom, and I see from *Who's Who* that there is a Sir Graham Latimer there who became the President of the Maori Council, so perhaps he is a distant cousin of mine, and Isaac's enthusiasm lives on in his brother's great-grandson. Isaac was proud of being unaffected by seasickness and that he had gathered together eight other non-sufferers on the first Sunday at sea, to sing from *Hymns Ancient and Modern* in the saloon for two hours accompanied by an 'extra young lady' on the ship's organ. One has to admire the Victorians for their sheer stamina. The advent of refrigeration was, at that time, ending the economic depression in New Zealand by making it possible to export frozen mutton; *Arawa* was able to provide her passengers and crew with fresh meat and vegetables from her own refrigerators, much to Isaac's delight. He seems to have been as busy at table as everywhere else.

After we had been in Tenerife for a few days, George, Muriel, Bill and I made an expedition to Orotava. Rastus came with us to deal with the taxi driver who took us there, and it must have been a squash in the car. While we were waiting at a bus stop for our homeward journey we entered into conversation with a policeman – I suppose a *guardia civil* – with one of those wooden hats flattened at the back. He was carrying, or rather dragging, a rifle, and he complained bitterly about how hard he found 'the service'. Encounters of this sort colour one's impressions more than they should. Whenever I see any reference to Spanish police, I think of this fellow – he was the only Spanish policeman I have ever talked to. Orotava was delightful, mild and balmy (Isaac had mentioned that the average temperature was 63.2 degrees in March). Inevitably we ended up sitting at a café, drinking coffee. Isaac spent much time in the Grand Hotel in Orotava, which had opened during the September before his visit. There had been a great celebration with a luncheon for 600, attended by the Prince of Brazil, who had come ashore from a Brazilian man-of-war lying in the port. Brazil became a republic soon after Isaac's time, but at the opening of the Grand Hotel there was still an Emperor and consequently a Prince.

Before we finally left Santa Cruz, Tim and I bought some 'delicacies'. With Rastus in attendance we went on a shopping expedition, each putting in £5 towards the cost. It says much for our beautiful natures that so far as I can recall we never fell out over the division of the various items: biscuits, cheese, tinned butter, porridge, crystallised fruits, nuts, dates, oranges, sardines, bully beef, strawberry jam, sultanas, raisins, and a small jar of pâté de foie gras. These were all in very small quantities and had disappeared by the time we had crossed the Atlantic. I do however recollect one source of particular annoyance in connection with beer. This was a special problem on board AA because it's not much fun drinking beer in the tropics unless it is really cold. Our only method of cooling beer was to put the bottle or can into the strictly limited space of a small paraffin-operated refrigerator which was secured at the bottom of the main companionway leading down to the central accommodation where our two couples had their cabins. It was of course accessible to all. The beer needed to be in the refrigerator for about three hours before it became thoroughly cold. On a couple of occasions, when I took my bottle out (I favoured Amstel lager), I found that it had been replaced by a warm one. I never found out who was playing this low trick; it turned out to be the worst thing that happened on the passage to Barbados.

On the morning of our departure, as we made ready to cast off, an odd thing occurred. We were waiting for a Belgian passenger ship to leave from the other side of the harbour, in order not to cramp its movements. Jim and I were standing in the bow while he explained to me what the crew of the Belgian were doing and why. She was lifting her anchor, which she had dropped in the harbour to keep her head away from the quayside. As the dripping cable emerged, to the accompaniment of a regularly dinging bell indicating the fathoms recovered, Jim told me that when the anchor was up and housed, she would move off, having let go aft. Out came the anchor and, just as it was about to house itself, it suddenly fell off the end of its cable and back into the water with a great splash. Jim was amazed. 'The Mate'll get big stick for that,' he said, as the ship moved out, leaving its anchor at the bottom of the harbour, presumably to be recovered later.

I can't leave Tenerife without a final word about Rastus. The evening before we left, we – that is, a part of the crew whose constituents I can no longer remember – had a meal in Santa Cruz, to which he was invited. We tried to make it something special, with good wine, even though we couldn't afford a first-class restaurant. As we were leaving the next morning, there was Rastus on the quayside to say goodbye. I think he was sad to see us go as he stood there in his crumpled suit, once-white nylon shirt and lemon-coloured tie. I will never be able to think of Tenerife without also thinking of Rastus. He was always so polite and well-mannered, but it was impossible to tell what he really thought of us. We were clearly neither merchant seamen nor yacht people; perhaps that is why he found us interesting. I have no idea what he did before we arrived or after we left – it is as if he had been invented purely for the period of our visit. It has always been an enigma to me, but he certainly eased our problems in Santa Cruz, and we were grateful.

* * * * *

Once at sea again we expected, or at least I did, that we would soon pick up the northeast trade wind, but that is not the way of it. I have no doubt that most people who have waited impatiently for the trades must have thought that they were unusually delayed, on the principle of the watched pot that never boils. In our case we did not pick them up until we were south of the Tropic of Cancer, at about Latitude 21 degrees north, and Longitude 22 degrees west. For the first three days after our departure we motored in light airs from the north. AA rolled of course, but not heavily, which encouraged us to bring our deck chairs onto the foredeck and to sprawl about in the sunshine, to the point where Nigel was obliged to growl from his seat at the wheel, 'Just like Daddy's yacht'. It was at this time that afternoon tea was inaugurated. Every afternoon at four o'clock there would be a tea party on the foredeck. I believe Muriel was the instigator: she made a large pot of tea for whoever was free to join the group. I would produce a tin of Carr's biscuits (strictly rationed). Muriel was teaching herself to play the mandolin. There had been some misgivings about this, but in fact she played quite well, if hesitantly, accompanying herself with a perfectly adequate voice. George would bring up his personal chair, which was really a rocking chair chocked against rocking, and would sit in it alongside the port bulwark facing forward, watching the passing sea, just like a man on a bus.

In Corunna Jim had started a navigation class in the aft cabin in the evenings. This had become very popular, with Nigel, Bill, Tim, Pam and one or two others on a floating basis. Nigel was, I think, the most assiduous pupil, giving the subject the close attention and concentration that he brought to everything he did. In spite of having been taught navigation at school I knew it was not my forte and I didn't attend. I sold my sextant later, but meanwhile I lent it to someone who wanted to learn. These classes now began to bear fruit, with a navigation group forming up on the foredeck every day at noon for the midday sights. The noon position line would be run on to the evening star sight, and the most proficient navigator was the one who put the ship closest to Jim's official position. Tim would spend much time with his telescope studying the sky at night. Occasionally he would let others look through it, and one night I arrived on watch to find that he and Nigel had been looking at the first sight of the Southern Cross, low above the horizon to the south. This was a moving occasion for Nigel; it meant he was heading home, to familiar sights.

This short period of peaceful weather ended suddenly on March 19th when the wind backed slightly to the north and strengthened to force 6 to 7, heralding an unpleasant three to four days of real discomfort. Our course lay roughly southwest, and with a fresh to strong wind from the north it will be plain to anyone who has experienced conditions at sea in a small powerboat with the wind broad on the quarter, that we were uncomfortable. AA, being underballasted, treated us to a quick, jerky, corkscrew motion peculiarly her own. She went back to her old trick of picking up a large dollop of sea in her scuppers, transferring it across her deck and then, before it had time to escape, flinging it back across the deck again. I could swear that we tossed the same portion of sea backwards and forwards across our deck for hundreds of miles. The galley was a dreadful place to be, while the wheelhouse, being the highest part of her structure, was the most unpleasant place of all. The helmsman had to hang onto the wheel, and could hardly maintain his perch on the seat – a sort of padded high stool fixed to the wheelhouse floor. Our mizzen sail helped slightly to dampen the speed of her roll, but we could not use any other sails, so we had to put up with this until we picked up the trade wind on March 23rd.

The arrival of the trades was dramatic. At first I was very disappointed, thinking that we had been cheated. The wind veered to northeast by east, but discouragingly light. We set all our sails – twin staysails, mizzen, mizzen topsail (the old patched mizzen hung upside down) and the big jib boomed out to starboard. We wallowed along at about two knots. The crew shook their heads: George said 'At this rate we'll starve before we get to Barbados.' I felt a bit of a fool and went to my bunk that night in a state of gloom. I woke up to go on watch at midnight and was immediately aware of a change in AA's motion. She was plunging heavily and I could hear a loud chuckling of water behind the bow planking, close to my head. I climbed out onto the foredeck to see that the sky was cloudless, a mass of stars which reeled about our mastheads as AA lurched forward; she was certainly sailing. Every sail and sheet cracked and strained in a strong northeaster; in the darkness she seemed to fly down the wind like an old tea clipper, rolling and heaving to the accompaniment of a melancholy chime as the ship's bell hanging in front of the wheelhouse tapped lightly on its clapper.

I staggered around the deck, delighted, checking the sheets to make sure that nothing was about to carry away, then climbed into the wheelhouse where Nigel was on the helm. I felt vindicated: 'How about that, then?' 'Must be doing all of five knots,' he said. But AA had taken on a new life, and in the dim light of the navigation lights I could see the foam passing as if we were competing for the America's Cup. A hallucination! Our day's run at noon was 113 miles, so Nigel wasn't far out. That proved to be one of our best days, but on several occasions we topped 100 miles. That would do – we could manage with that. As life settled into a trade-wind routine the only disadvantage to having the engine stopped was that we were unable to collect hot washing-up water from the engine exit pipe by dangling a bucket under it.

A great deal has been written about trade-wind sailing, and I have read a great deal of it. Between the ages of about 11 and 16 I read little else but sea stories, of which the most memorable were those of Captain F. C. Hendry, writing under the pen-name Shalimar. He wrote from direct experience, having served as an apprentice on the great four-masted barques which traded to Chile to load nitrates for the European fertiliser market at the end of the 19th century. Later he had worked as a pilot in the Far East and on freighters all over the place, but my favourites were the stories about the barques on their dangerous voyages round Cape Horn to Iquique and Valparaiso. Of all his books the one I admired most – I have read it three times – was *A Windjammer's Half-Deck*, a tragic tale containing his memories of sailing in the northeast trades.

> *The seaman's paradise, where the wind hardly varies half a point in direction, or a knot in strength, and braces, halyards and sheets are rarely touched for days on end ... the sun climbed higher into the heavens, but the weather never became very hot; the fresh trade wind kept the atmosphere deliciously cool. The sky was blue save for the fleecy trade wind clouds; the sea bluer still, with white foam like delicate lace on the wave crests ... The hum of the wind in the rigging was like sweet music, the splash of the spreading bow wave and the swish of the passing water soothed and lulled.*

It is not surprising that I longed to be in this enchanted part of the world and to experience these delights. It was all just as Shalimar described; I was not in the slightest disappointed.

With the trade wind came the dolphins, playing around our bows, twisting and turning as if showing off their agility, seeming to enjoy our slowness as it made them even more brilliant by contrast. I spent long periods leaning over the bows watching them, particularly during the half-light when they were outlined in phosphorescence like ghosts. In full darkness their bodies were covered in phosphorescent bubbles, greenish and unearthly.

At the other end of AA, fishing went on with a strong atmosphere of competition. It was acknowledged by all fair-minded members of the crew that John was the best and most successful fisherman, but this was not always admitted by some, and never by Nigel. Fishing was done by three different methods. Firstly by line over the stern – fairly successful but not requiring much skill. Secondly by spear gun, which was not successful at all; refraction made it difficult to aim the gun accurately. Thirdly by gaffing over the side, at which John was expert, having the required speed and accuracy. He would hover at the ship's side, with gaff poised over the gunwale, striking with a lightning stroke when an unwary dorado presented itself within range. Nigel emulated him, but lacked the split-second decision-making skill. I told him that he took too long to get ready; he replied that John was almost as quick to strike as he was to put the bite on someone for a cigarette.

We saw no other ships. The days were long gone when trade-wind routes were crowded with sailing vessels, while steamships used the shortest, great circle routes, as one would expect. We felt strangely isolated in our circle of ocean, with its consistent skyscape of small fluffy clouds lining the horizon. The waves alongside seemed familiar, like water in a rock pool, while the quartering wave set up by our movement through the sea acquired an intimate character of its own, forever curling and tumbling as if trying to keep up with us but falling back defeated. We moved as if in a dream. Quite apart from the pleasure of watching the dolphins, there was something mesmerising about the pushing of our forefoot through the water. It reminded me of a description of the forward movement of the bows of a freighter that I had read long before in a novel by H. M. Tomlinson. I had to wait until I was back in England before finding it again. It came from *Galleon's Reach*, published in 1927: 'The cutwater of the ship was deep and plain in the blue transparency, coming along with unvarying confidence like the nose of an exploring monster.' It was the fault of these various writers, and my avid reading, that I was on *Aberdeen Anzac* at all.

Reading is an important resource on a long passage, which is why I had prepared a tiny library of esteemed literature – the type of books which I ought to have read, had not yet got round to, but now would. As George was interested in reading them too we made a literary circle of two, with Jim on the periphery. Les had the distinction of being the only one on board who was able to read Patrick White's *Voss*, which had been enjoying, if that is the right word, a vogue before we had left England. One saw him with the book, clutching his head, but mercifully it disintegrated as soon as he had finished it, so we were spared the ordeal. That is to say, the book disintegrated, not his head. In the aft cabin several paperbacks lay about, becoming grubbier and more dog-eared until they disappeared into the gash bucket and over the side, but my hardback classics were preserved and I still have them. George and I read *The Mill on the Floss* and *Adam Bede* in succession and exchanged views. Our criticism was desultory and largely made up of comments on the characters. George would sit in his rocking chair by the bulwarks and say, for example, apropos *Adam Bede*, 'What's all this about paper hats? When did carpenters wear paper hats?' I couldn't help him except that I remembered an illustration by Tenniel in *Alice Through the Looking Glass* showing the carpenter, in 'The Walrus and the Carpenter', wearing what I supposed was a paper hat: that mollified him.

The Mill on the Floss was spoilt for me by the ending. It was not that I objected to the drowning of Maggie and

Tom – that seemed tragically apposite – but I found the manner and description of their deaths absurd. There they were, out on the flood in their rowing boat, when they were run down by a mass of timber made up of the remains of some 'wooden machinery' being carried along in the current. For some inexplicable reason this machinery was travelling much faster than Tom and Maggie's boat, although common sense would dictate that they would all have been travelling along at the same speed. Ineptly, they collide with it and are drowned. It seemed to me that George Eliot had resolved on their despatch together, not being too careful about the means.[1]

George and I then moved on to Conrad's *Under Western Eyes*, which we enjoyed while agreeing that it was about 50,000 words too long. Upon re-reading I still think it is too long but I would rather read a too-long Conrad book than nearly anyone else's work of the correct length. It seems that once he had started a book he didn't know when to stop, nor did he have any idea how long it was going to be when he started, but went on until he was exhausted and ill.

Sometimes, while talking to George, or to anyone else who happened to be around, I would work on the sails, repairing the seams or bolt-ropes, or would wander around coiling down lines in pathetic attempts to make AA seem more yacht-like. George would mock my efforts from his rocking chair: a pointless effort, he would say. He was right. There was absolutely nothing of the yacht about AA; she was an affair of clanging steel doors, rough wood surfaces, vertical metal ladders and the crude strength of a North Sea trawler. I had sailed in proper yachts: one in

---

[1] On reading John Sutherland's book *Who Betrays Elizabeth Bennet?* (1999), I find that George Eliot knew more about hydrodynamics than I do. It seems that a flooded river meeting an incoming tide can create complex and powerful swirls and counter-currents, and these could have swept Tom's boat into wooden structures being dragged along by the undertow. I am still left wondering why he didn't try to row out of the way.

particular, Ivan Carr's *Solway Maid*, the last-built of William Fife's creations, a most beautiful vessel, and would sometimes think of her, disloyally, with nostalgia. I compared AA's performance with what I imagined would have been *Solway Maid*'s ten-knot onward rush. AA lurched. She had an odd characteristic which I had not encountered before but which may not be uncommon. She would roll vigorously for several minutes, with increasing violence; then suddenly stop for a short time before starting the cycle again. It was almost as if she recognised that she was going too far, making us too uncomfortable, so desisted for a moment out of very shame.

Jim and his sight-takers became inured to this motion which made navigation sessions difficult. The whole procedure of celestial navigation is impressive and magical – I could recognise this even though I took no part myself. The punctual and precise appearance of the heavenly bodies on which we depended was reassuring. It was like – is like – being inside a huge and perfect clock. I was reminded of this stately progress of the heavens many years later when I was talking to a farmer in the Vale of Lorton, in the Lake District. His farm lay in the shadow of a craggy outcrop so that throughout the winter the greater part of it received no direct sunlight. He always knew when spring had come because on a particular day, sunlight entered a certain window for the first time in the year. This he found heartening and it reconciled him to the long dark winter months. A special seriousness attached to navigation which increased with our distance from land. Nobody made jokes about the star sights. It was as if the line up with sextants was part of some sacerdotal function, a priestly rite.

One evening, as Nigel sat in the loo, with the door open, a flying fish flew in through the doorway, grazed his leg and thudded against the bulkhead beside him. They often came aboard, attracted, I believe, by our deck lights.

Occasionally we would cook and eat the largest, but on the whole we didn't bother – they were too small. Our principal fish resource was the dorado, a rather dull fish which Pam and Muriel were hard put to present in palatable form. We had dorado with rice and pineapple, not because it was remarkably attractive, but because we had plenty of rice and tinned pineapple – I think Les had secured a bulk order of the latter at a very favourable price. We also had plenty of tinned pork and tinned beef – served with rice of course. In an attempt to vary our diet, fishing intensified, but nothing ever seemed to be caught that was edible apart from the boring, chewy dorado. John held the record, with a 19 lb example.

A horrible-looking hammerhead shark was caught once with a line over the stern. It fought fiercely on the afterdeck, with blood all over the place, until it was despatched with a hatchet. It was of course quite inedible. Nigel nearly caught a monster, the stuff of nightmares, on a trailing line, but didn't get it on board. Nobody knew what it was, and it grew vastly in the telling to the point where some doubted that it had existed at all; but I had seen something, dimly, on his line in our wake, something terrifyingly large and sinister, and I was glad that it had escaped. There is something peculiarly chilling and unnerving about the glimpse of a large predatory fish under the surface of the water which no doubt explains the great success of the film *Jaws*. In my own case, I can date this fear to my first sight, on page 40 of Beatrix Potter's *Tale of Jeremy Fisher*, of the picture of a large trout's head about to seize Jeremy's leg. On another occasion, John caught something called a snake haddock, evil-looking like so many of the creatures which emerge from the deep. The aft deck was the main scene of fishing activity, but there was a special reservation for Nigel's homemade deck chair, where he liked to relax after his evening meal, watching our phosphorescent wake and looking at stars through Tim's

Jim and Bill painting
Aberdeen Anzac's
registration.

Taking on fuel
at Shoreham,
October 1959.

From the top,
Dick, Keith and
Dave in Shoreham,
October 1959.

Aberdeen Anzac
rolling in
the Atlantic

On the beach
at Corunna,
December 1959.

Celebration dinner,
Corunna, December
1959. Bill, Muriel,
Dave and Jim.

An important discussion at Corunna. C.A.L. wants Bill to help him,
but he won't. Nor will Les or Tim.

Nigel and Tim.

Jim with
Mohican haircut.

Nigel navigating.

Jim and C.A.L. rigging
twin staysails to take
advantage of the
trade winds.

Nigel, hanging
out his washing.

Muriel, about to delight a small audience in the Atlantic. She is sitting in George's rocking chair.

Dave playing his guitar, well away from everyone else.

Flying fish.

The big jib at work.

George and Les in Barbados. They've just finished clearing up the deck.

John with a fish. Nigel said, 'Because he's holding it, doesn't mean he caught it.'

Aberdeen Anzac in the Panama Canal.

Election day, Galapagos.

Ua Pou in the Marquesas.

Polynesian children,
Moorea.

Dancer,
Tahiti.

Dick with
his engine.

Moorea,
July 1960.

Les has found
New Zealand
in the atlas.

Aberdeen Anzac arriving in Auckland.

Clearing customs in Auckland.

In Auckland. Back row (L-R): Les, C.A.L., Jim, Tim, Bill, Dick. In front: Dave, George, Pam, Muriel.

telescope. I spent more time at the other end of the ship, sometimes hanging over the bows to watch the dolphins, if they were visiting, and listening to the sighing sound as they breathed through the holes in the backs of their heads.

Dick and Jim both became very interested in sailing, while Dick in particular would come round with me to deal with chafe by wrapping the sheets in pieces of rag. We couldn't afford to allow any cordage to chafe through because we had no spare to draw upon. I managed a couple of splices – a back splice and a long splice – having dimly remembered how to do them from my school days. They were lumpy and unprofessional, but adequate. Then my fingers gave up: there used to be a saying among sailors, 'every finger a marlin spike', but that was not true in my case. We all admired Nigel's spar, the one that he had made to boom out our big jib, and he went on to fashion other wooden fittings. He spent some time working on fife rails to secure lines inside the bulwarks on both sides of AA – he relished this work. Once I looked into his leather tool bag, congratulating him on the perfect condition of the contents. He said that the next time I went on an ocean voyage not to forget the man with a bag of tools. 'Never mind the romantic stuff, just look in his tool bag – it'll tell you all you need to know.'

* * * * *

So our days went peacefully by as we ran down the trade-wind route. We weren't bored; there seemed to be a continual supply of diversions, many of them trivial, such as my noticing that the snouts of the dolphin were like the nozzle covers for Calor gas bottles. In the circumscribed world of shipboard life small things become important. Dick, with his engine silenced, became more communicative and talked about motor cycles, which were of particular interest to him. We discussed sailing and speculated on various ways in which we might squeeze another quarter of a knot out of AA. He hated to be idle. It was Dick who had himself trailed over the side for a swim when our speed fell to the point when it was safe to do so; nobody else was tempted. Jim, John and Dave shaved each other's heads shortly after we left Santa Cruz and they looked very odd. I suppose the reason was that they wanted to cool their heads and didn't want to have to wash their hair. I told them that they would regret it when they got to Barbados where they would attract unwelcome attention from the Barbadians, as freaks. As a consequence of being isolated from the world, incarcerated together on AA, the characteristics of the crew became more clearly defined, or perhaps the truth was that they became more noticeable to others. John, for example, became known as Eccentric John, and this was before he had his head shaved, having earned the name on account of some quirks of dress. His hat, in order to secure it, he had attached by a long piece of string the other end of which was tied to his belt at the back. His plimsolls being too small, he had cut off the front part in order to save the cost of new ones. Strict economy was necessary – he had to have enough money to buy cigarettes.

Pam and Muriel were comparatively unchanged in appearance, although neither was at the cutting edge of fashion. There had been by this time some change in the galley routine, which had been based on the original arrangement of alternating duties, day and day about, shared by Pam and Muriel, with one of the crew to help. At some point Dave had revealed that he used to work in a bakery; a surprise to all, but Dave was full of surprises. He offered to bake our bread, so the galley was handed over to him for the morning for the mysterious ceremony of bread making. The mystery arose in large part from the isolation he insisted upon. Nobody was allowed in the galley while his work went forward – not even to open the door –

otherwise the batch he was making would be ruined. He talked about 'knocking back', and Bill said that he didn't know what Dave was knocking back in there, but that he, Bill, would like to have some of it. The end product, six fine loaves, was very welcome as an addition to our tea parties, eaten with jam or peanut butter. I volunteered to make porridge for breakfast; it fitted in with my coming off duty at 8.00 a.m. and made a pleasant and aromatic start to the day.

I mentioned earlier that Jim was on the periphery of George's and my book critics' circle. He read quickly but erratically, with little apparent discrimination, but he certainly enjoyed *Dr. Thorne*. He also admired *Lord Jim*, having a professional appreciation of the issues involved in the story. I asked him what he was laughing about as he lay in his bunk reading it, not being able to think of any laughs in that book. He read me out the passage about the attitude of the British Merchant Service officers in the Far East: 'They now had a horror of the home service, with its harder conditions, severer view of duty, and the hazard of stormy seas. They were attuned to the eternal peace of eastern sky and sea. They loved short passages, good deck chairs, large native crews, and the distinction of being white.' 'He's right about that,' said Jim, 'the distinction of being white. Oh yes, there was a lot to be said for that. He must have known all about that in his day, and it was true in my day, too.' When he'd finished the book, we talked about it. There was one particular aspect of the story that puzzled me, which we were never able to resolve. Those who have read *Lord Jim* will remember that Jim's ship, the *Patna*, is abandoned by her officers, including Jim, when they think she is about to founder following a collision with some unspecified underwater hazard. They are swept astern of the *Patna* in their lifeboat by a squall which blows just at the moment of their departure and swings *Patna* head to wind. As she swings – and this is vital to the understanding of events – her navigation lights are occluded and therefore cannot be seen by those in the lifeboat, because they only show from dead ahead to two points aft of the beam on either side. So, they see no lights and assume that she has gone down with a rush, which is what they were expecting. Fair enough, but what happened to her stern light which by maritime law she was obliged to show at her stern and which they should have seen? Conrad does not explain this. Jim (our Jim, that is) said that maybe *Patna* was so far down by the head that the light was shining up into the sky and so wouldn't have been seen from the lifeboat. I thought that was not a satisfactory explanation. It was only her forepeak which had been flooded, which would not have lifted her stern to that extent, so they should have seen the light. Our wrangling about it so seriously is, I suppose, the mark of a great work of fiction. It still worries me after all these years. If I could get Conrad back for half an hour to ask him one question, that is the one I would ask. Jim gave it as his opinion that Lord Jim had done a dreadful thing in abandoning the ship, although he had sympathy for him, and hoped that he, Jim, would never be put to the test in that way.

Muriel evidently had a birthday during the Atlantic crossing, because Nigel wrote in a letter to Jean that she 'was tickled with her rose made of green crepe toilet paper, and shortly, at 4.00 p.m. we'll try the birthday cake Pam is making.' The letter is dated April 1st, unfortunate for Muriel, but whatever the date the scope for finding presents was limited. Nigel no doubt made the rose himself so it would have been well constructed.

We had been under sail alone for twelve days when the trade wind lightened to the point where our speed dropped to less than three knots. AA heaved and wallowed, with new noises making themselves heard. For some reason our reduced progress altered our roll, setting up fresh chatters, clanks and thumps. The anchor shank, which was stowed under the trawling winch just forward of the wheelhouse and perfectly quiet until now, started to clink with our roll so that the noise became the dominant sound of the night watches. We were able to measure our speed by dropping empty beer cans over the bow and timing them with a stop watch as they came into line with our counter. Jim said that that would never have done on the B.I. cadet ship, but, like Muriel with her rose, he was tickled by the primitive but accurate device.

Any reader might suppose, having read to this point, that Tim's activities were limited to watching the night sky through his telescope, but this was far from the case. As our radio officer, his principal duty was to provide us with a time signal which he gave to Jim each morning before noon sights. That, and receiving *The Archers* for Pam and Muriel. About halfway across the Atlantic *The Archers* faded away. We were, putting it at its least, not well-provided in radio facility; the radio had been put out of action when the wheelhouse was flooded during the hurricane. It was repaired under our insurance claim in Corunna, but it was inadequate for any real service – it had, after all, been made for use in an army tank – so we could not rely on it. Tim as one of our engineers was also responsible for monitoring our fuel consumption, keeping records of hours run, as well as doing normal engine-room watch duty. He also monitored Nigel and John, acting as minder for both, umpiring cigarette consumption, arbitrating in disputes – all in all, very demanding work. Enforcing economy became one of his main responsibilities. Economy, to Nigel, John, and Tim, *was* cigarettes. Nigel would look witheringly at John as he lit another (I believe John smoked more than anyone else) and say, 'My God, he's weak.' John: 'At least it's one of my own.' Nigel: 'Yes, you've finished mine,' and so on. I would pretend not to listen to these exchanges, which I enjoyed very much, because I knew that they would be in purer form if there was no consciousness of an audience.

It was at about this time that Muriel and Pam began making chutney. Improbable as it seems, yet that is what my salt-stained notes tell me, and I was certainly not in the mood to invent things. I think that events that are important at the time, important enough to write down under inconvenient circumstances, are often not the things that seem natural to record, when read many years later. Sometimes my own notes puzzle me, or are incomprehensible. For example I find in my notebook, one of those spiral-bound St George notebooks 'for Shorthand; for Reporters; for Schools', the words 'lemon curd' heavily underlined. Very significant in mid-Atlantic 44 years ago but the reason for this will never be recovered. The foregoing is incidental to the important fact that Pam and Muriel did make chutney. They were extremely good-natured, those two, sharing the galley without complaint – or none that I heard – and making the best of pathetically limited provisions. Pam had become swept up in the general enthusiasm for navigation and took part in the daily sight taking. Muriel played her mandolin. Dave had a guitar which he played in a different part of the ship – sitting on the grating over the steering gear, right aft.

It was, I believe, a pleasant time for all. At our tea parties, though we had soon finished my two tins of Carr's fancy biscuits, we had Dave's bread with jam or honey. As we edged south and the heat became too great during the middle of the day, Nigel erected a personalised shelter which he described to Jean in a letter: 'The weather is of course very hot now but I've sewn together a few old sails and odd pieces of canvas and made an awning to throw shade over the stern. I have a small vice there and am quite happy in the shade working or reading – or just sitting!' At our end of the ship, Jim and I had suffered from stuffiness in our cabin, so had contrived a wind scoop to channel air down the hatchway. This was helped by a down-draught from the twin headsails when they were set, but when the wind died it became nearly insupportable in the fo'c'sle. The long spell of fine clear weather began to break up in rain squalls as we neared Barbados.

Our deck planking, shrunken in the heat, let the water through onto our bunks and caused much annoyance. To quote Nigel again: 'During the night I found tacks and a hammer and fixed the two most annoying leaks – nailed a thick sock over one and a khaki woollen hat over the other and then slept soundly until morning.' Not being blessed with Nigel's inventiveness or initiative, I covered myself with an oilskin coat and put up with the drips until the planking swelled again.

Twenty-three days out of Santa Cruz, during which time we had not seen a single vessel, we sighted Barbados. Thanks to Jim, the island was exactly where it should have been. It presented the odd sight of emperor palms sticking as if out of the water, a line of them, tossing in the wind. We dropped our anchor and waited for clearance, feeling dazed with wind and sun, pleased with ourselves and confident that we were 'getting on'.

Barbados in 1960 was heaving and throbbing with the sound of steel bands. It was everywhere, leaking out of houses, shops, bars; it even seemed to be coming up out of the pavement. Our berth in Bridgetown harbour was noisy and cluttered with small local craft to the extent that we didn't want to stay there longer than necessary. There was shopping to do, a task that fell largely on Pam and Muriel. I was anxious to get my laundry done and that turned out to be as big a problem as it had been in Corunna. There, I had given it to a professed laundry woman who returned it in due course with about one third of the clothes missing. I asked Tim, with his adequate Spanish, to remonstrate with her on my behalf. He and she had a long conversation, which when translated to me threw an interesting light on the attitude of disadvantaged Spanish women living in a large industrial port. She freely admitted that she had sold some of my clothes, but she was a widow with two children to bring up and was finding it hard to survive. Her life was very hard – she had to do what she could to augment her income. As we were more fortunate than she was it was natural that she should try to make a bit extra out of us. She made no apology but said she probably would not have done it if it had not been for her children. I could do nothing in the face of such frank admission, so I told her, through Tim, that though I did not grudge her the extra money she had made I was sure she would understand that I would now use another washerwoman. I felt like Don Quixote; I found this plain Spanish speaking rather refreshing, although I would have appreciated it more if it had not involved my clothes.

In Barbados also I suffered from a washerwoman.

There was a strong egalitarian atmosphere in the place. The woman who took my laundry evidently believed in garment redistribution. She was less ingenuous than the one in Corunna, claiming that she had returned exactly the same clothes that I had given her, or if she hadn't someone must have stolen them when she wasn't looking. It quickly became apparent that I wasn't going to get any redress, so after this episode I made do with fewer clothes and washed them myself.

I came upon this same liking for equality when I went to get a shave in a barber's shop. The barber didn't want to shave me because, as he said, Barbadians shaved themselves. I told him that I was living on a small boat, that fresh water was precious, that in any case I was not a Barbadian. He agreed to shave me, as a favour, and having settled the point to his satisfaction became quite friendly.

I spent some time overhauling our sails, which had suffered little during the crossing. Sitting on the deck under an awning which extended either side of the wheelhouse structure was pleasant, watching the passing scene, even though the noise was prodigious. A short distance from AA there was a little square, with a statue of Lord Nelson in the middle. This puzzled me, as I didn't understand why he should be commemorated in Barbados, or, if it had seemed appropriate to do so in earlier days, why the new West Indian Confederation had not pulled him down. I was ignorant, not being aware that in 1960 Barbados was still under British rule. But, more than this, it had not occurred to me how much the whole of South and Central America owed to Nelson. After Trafalgar, at which he destroyed the Spanish battle fleet, the colonies were able to break free from Spanish rule; so Nelson could be seen as the champion of the new republics of South America, although I doubt if he would have seen his role in that light, convinced Tory that he was. More than this, I had not realised that Barbados had been saved from falling into

French hands by Nelson and Cochrane, so it was not surprising that Nelson's statue should commemorate him in Bridgetown.

There was a strangely aimless atmosphere in Bridgetown, as if everybody was waiting for something to happen, or not to happen, and it didn't matter which. Perhaps they were waiting for independence, which was imminent. There was a bird heard everywhere which made a hot airless sound, like someone blowing across the top of a milk bottle. Descending into our cabin was like entering a Turkish bath. News was of race riots in South Africa and trouble in Notting Hill. A black cat with a three-cornered head glared at me out of a shop window, and the indistinct way of speaking among the townspeople made it difficult to understand what they were saying. All in all, I think we were glad when Pam and Muriel had finished their shopping so that we could motor across to Kingstown, St Vincent, which we found to be more congenial and peaceful. Not altogether peaceful at night however. Warring tribes of dogs in the town became active after nightfall, maintaining savage battle until the small hours. On our first night, April 13th, I lay awake listening to this dreadful noise until about 2.00 a.m., when it was suddenly interrupted by the prolonged hoarse squealing of a pig, followed by silence.

The following day Bill and I set off on foot to explore the town and its surroundings. First we went to Barclay's Bank which was the only place I knew to be air-conditioned. There I sat and read their copy of *The Times* for half an hour in the blessed cool, while Bill, who was made of sterner stuff, walked about in the sun. When he had rejoined me we visited the cathedral, very quietly, as there was a service in progress. Feeling self-conscious when all the congregation turned their heads to look at us, we made a circuit of the aisles to examine the wall memorials, which are always interesting and informative.

One of them commemorated the life of Major Dalzell of the Royal Fusiliers, who had been assassinated in 1824. What had been going on in 1824? A riot? A crazed soldier, driven beyond endurance by harsh discipline in a hot climate? I never found out, and remain puzzled. Feeling thirsty, we went into a bar. As soon as we entered, the few men standing around drinking fell silent and stared at us. It was most unnerving, so we had a quick beer and left. It was like going onto a film set where a violent scene is about to take place which we had interrupted. We walked on until we came to an old fort, built in the days of the continual struggles between the British and the French and which had no doubt been garrisoned by both sides as the fortunes of war swung back and forth. Nature was taking over. The scene prompted reflections on the transitoriness of power and Empire, so we reflected for a few minutes. As we walked back to the harbour I noticed an advertisement announcing '555 State Express: The Queen Smokes Them.' I told Nigel about this, but he wasn't impressed.

It had never been our intention to stay for long in Kingstown. We wanted a peaceful anchorage in flat water so that we could start our repainting: first the wheelhouse structure, then the hull. When on April 15th we moved across to Admiralty Bay in Bequia we found it was ideal for our purpose. Bequia was idyllic. We anchored close to the shore in gin-clear water, in colour a mixture of turquoise and emerald. Leaning over the bow to check that our anchor was lying well, I could follow the chain by eye clearly down to the CQR biting into the multi-coloured seabed. The colours were amazing – it was like being part of a travel brochure, although I imagine that anyone taking a photograph to advertise the West Indies would have preferred a white yacht in the foreground rather than AA's homely presence.

Those who find AA an object of interest will like to

know that her colour scheme was destined for change. Her deck structure, the steel part of her, was to be painted a pale powder-blue. This was not so much a matter of aesthetic choice as of necessity: we had on board a large quantity of powder-blue paint. No doubt Les had been able to pick up a job lot cheap, or possibly without paying for it at all. As anyone who has painted steel will know, most of the work is preparatory. There were many hours of tedious chipping with special hammers in order to remove the old paint. I did not like this work, doing as little as I possibly could, but Jim did. It may have reminded him of his cadet days in the B.I. Company. He made himself an odd sun hat with a handkerchief arranged round the back of his neck, which gave him the appearance of a Foreign Legionnaire, a character from *Beau Geste*, as he stood for hours with his mind in neutral, chipping away. Dave helped him, and others joined in from time to time, but no one was as assiduous as Jim. He was, no doubt about it, a many-faceted character. His liking for paint chipping bordered on addiction, which was just as well as it had to be done.

Dave had stopped making bread by this time so Tim went ashore every morning to place an order with the local bakery. This was presided over by a large and somewhat domineering woman who questioned poor Tim about his churchgoing habits. Tim was obliged to admit that he did not make a regular attendance. Easter loomed; the baker insisted that Tim should go to the local church where the Church of the West Indies (Anglican) would be holding a big service. Tim demurred but she would have none of that and made him promise to go. She did not quite say that our bread supply depended on his going, but it was clear that relations would be badly soured if he didn't. So he promised, and got me to agree to come with him. On Easter Sunday we put on our best clothes and walked up to the attractive white-painted church which stood above the bay. I'm very glad we did – it was a splendid occasion. The church was packed, almost entirely with women and children. The women were magnificently dressed, most of them with large hats. I saw only two or three men. The priest was white, dressed up in exquisite robes, with a white ruff round his neck. All was done with meticulous care and precision, the child servitors performing their duties impeccably. Singing was loud and enthusiastic, as one would imagine, and everybody was very happy. The baker saw us and gave Tim a huge welcoming smile. The service seemed to me to be middle-of-the-road Anglican with a framework similar to that back in England, but with an entirely different and much more exuberant spirit. The next day, Easter Monday, was treated as a day of celebration with dancing and a cricket match.

The village clustered at the edge of Admiralty Bay. The centre of attraction to us was a shop with a large refrigerator in which beer, among other things, was stored. The industry of the island was – possibly still is – boat building, and we saw a number of black-hulled craft under construction on the beach. The foreman of the builders, as a mark of status, wore a bowler hat. He was rather tiresomely overbearing and self-important. Nobody doubted his pre-eminence but he wanted to make sure that it was recognised.

One day I took a short walk on an earth road, to the other side of the island. I found a completely deserted beach, about a mile long, with the surf rolling in onto firm sand. The only sign of human presence was a half-built schooner under a canopy of palm leaves, but no one in sight. I swam in the surf, thinking that this was all too good to be true, that there was bound to be a catch – sharks, jellyfish or at least a dead dolphin giving off a foul smell – but no, there were no disagreeable surprises and I was only driven by hunger to leave the place and walk back to Admiralty Bay. We made other short expeditions to various parts of the island, including a visit to a ship's chandler further along the coast, but we were in Bequia in order to paint AA so that is what we did most of the time. It's amazing how long it takes to paint a boat. Jim and Dave seemed perfectly happy to bear the bulk of this tedious task; even so I was a little ashamed of my small part in it.

Our dinghy has had little mention: it was badly damaged in the hurricane, repaired in Corunna and was stowed between the main hatch and the forward hatch. The longboat was not, to my recollection, ever used at all. It sat in its chocks over the aft cabin, a great heavy lump of a boat which, if we had launched it, would probably have sunk, its planking having opened up so much in the heat. In any case because of its weight we would have had to use the mizzen boom to launch it, a complicated operation, so there it sat, all the way from Southwick to Auckland. We had a circular inflatable life raft which was tested once, and then put away. It was not a satisfactory article, bought second-hand from some surplus store no doubt. But the little dinghy was greatly used, a fact which led to trouble later, but while at Bequia it was essential for ferrying us to and from the shore. It was very useful in topside painting. All in all it proved an invaluable tender, in contrast to the spurned longboat.

Goats and scratching hens, roaming unchecked, were a feature of Bequia. The continual trade wind induced a dreamy sensation; we loved the place. Sometimes there would be a cricket match to watch. At night, Tim would emerge with his telescope to study the stars – they were uncommonly bright – and speculate on their distance from the earth. We had delightful evenings on deck, a glass of rum and Coca-Cola in hand, looking forward to a dinner of spam Hawaii (spam, rice and tinned pineapple chunks), and if that does not sound enticing remember that menus are relative.

On the last day before our departure Dick, Bill and I

were rowing about in the dinghy when a 40-foot white yacht entered the bay and anchored a short distance from AA. The owner asked us to come aboard for a drink. He turned out to be a minister, I don't remember of what, representing St Vincent and the Grenadines in the newly formed West Indies Federation. He and his very pretty wife and a couple of chums were having a short cruise. I think the W.I.F. – long since defunct – was one of the stages on the road to full independence, but he was clearly a man of authority and decision, with high hopes for his department. We told him about our project; he studied AA through his binoculars and said that she was a fine ship, but that he'd rather stay with his own boat. It was the first time I had ever had a conversation with a West Indian politician. He was an impressive figure, and I have wondered since what became of him.

* * * * *

We sailed, very regretfully, on April 26th, reminding ourselves that we were supposed to be on the way to New Zealand. The wheelhouse was half orange undercoat and half powder-blue – I think Jim had finished chipping by this time. It had been our happiest visit. Nobody had stolen my laundry, or swindled us, while everywhere the people had been cheerful and friendly. We had learnt that there are great differences between the various peoples of the West Indian islands, of whom the Becquians must be among the most attractive.

We shaped a course for Curacao, where our next port of call was to be Willemstad, the capital. As we were still in the trade-wind area we set our rig for the passage of about 500 miles, motor-sailing with a light east wind, making about five knots. Our course took us close to the Islas las Aves not far from the coast of Venezuela. For some reason the memory of one of these little rocky islets, on which there was a very simple arrangement of lighthouse, dwelling and slipway, has stayed in my mind as sharp and clear as if I'd seen it yesterday. I can see it now, the little group baking in the sun without a soul in sight, as we rolled along, hearing the mild wash of the sea breaking on its beach. We studied it as usual through binoculars and speculated on the life of the lighthouse keeper in his domain.

Willemstad lies both sides of a waterway; our berth lay right beside a busy main street lined with utterly Dutch-style buildings – which is not surprising, bearing in mind that Curacao has been a Dutch possession since the seventeenth century, apart from a few short periods when it was held by Britain. Lying in our berth in the middle of Willemstad it seemed to me that we were in a very hot airless Amsterdam. This is where we planned to buy more diesel and put part of it into a dozen 40-gallon drums ranged inside the bulwarks on either side of AA. We needed to carry every drop we could in order to cover the distance to Tahiti, which would be our next opportunity to buy any – a long haul via the Galapagos and the Marquesas, part of which we knew we would have to sail. Diesel was comparatively cheap in Curacao – the place was dripping with oil brought over to the refineries from Venezuela.

The heat was oppressive so that sleep below was nearly impossible. I fixed up a bunk under the awning beside the wheelhouse and made frequent trips ashore to take cold showers at the Sailors' Home on the other side of the harbour. I spent much of my time in Willemstad under that shower. Another attraction of Willemstad was the existence of several very good restaurants providing the Indonesian cuisine which the Dutch had imported from their East Indian empire. We had two wonderful meals before parsimony inevitably took over. In 1960, the British Empire was being wound up, a disintegration in fits and starts which had been led by the departure from India in

1947. We had a good opportunity to see how the Dutch were coping, at least outwardly, with a similar situation, because the Queen of the Netherlands' birthday took place while we were there. There was to be a ceremony in the middle of the town, with full formality of parade, brass bands, the governor on a saluting base, in honour of Her Majesty, so Bill and I put on rather better clothes than usual and went along to see the show. The march past was of Dutch Marines and sailors of the Netherlands Navy, rather oddly pulling a field gun along behind them. They were dressed in their best uniforms, of course, sweltering in the heat and looking rather pale and ill, the officers carrying drawn swords. A band played a rousing march; the tramp of their boots together with the rumble of their gun was impressive, but I could not help reflecting that our fellows would have done it with more snap and verve. The commander of the naval contingent came forward, beaming, to shake hands with the Governor; a speech was made, and then they all marched away pulling their gun along behind them. It had been an old-fashioned occasion.

It had not occurred to me up to this point in our voyage that we were seen as objects of pity by anyone ashore, but it was in Willemstad that something happened to make me wonder. Dave was eating his breakfast, standing by the bulwarks facing the quayside, when suddenly a man who was passing leant over and gave him three bananas. I was close enough to this little scene to realise that it was a genuine act of charity, made not at all in the spirit of irony. The giver may have had the opportunity to examine Dave's breakfast, which was the porridge I had just made, so I was a little put out by the episode, as was Dave who just had sufficient presence of mind to thank his benefactor before he disappeared into the throng. Nigel, who had also witnessed the heart-warming exchange, swore that the very next morning he would eat his porridge in the same place and see what he could get.

Getting the extra fuel aboard in oil drums was heavy work, manhandling the drums from the quayside into position, six a side along the bulwarks, and lashing them securely against the rolling they would have to endure. We also took on board food stores, some of it in banana crates which we dumped on the foredeck preparatory to carrying them down into the lazarette. I picked up one of them to take it down the forehatch ladder. Out of it ran a large hairy-legged spider. Bill said, 'That's a tarantula.' I don't suppose he knew what a tarantula looked like and neither did I, but I wasn't going to argue about it so I dropped the box, picked up a dinghy oar and despatched the offending spider at the foot of the foremast. For a short time I was the hero of the Great Spider War, or the Spider Terror as it was sometimes called. Nigel told me I was very lucky: it could have jumped on me from six feet away and stung me to death before I had had time to shout 'Rule Britannia', he said.

Eventually all had been made ready for sea and we sailed on May 3rd, not sorry to say goodbye to such an oven-like place, with its spiders and smell of oil. As to spiders, I believe they came from Venezuela in the banana boxes, or amongst the bananas themselves, but it is characteristic of travel in general and of small-boat travel in particular, that a great deal of misinformation is imparted with vehement certitude, and for all I know the tarantula is indigenous to Curacao. To expand on the subject of inaccurate travel information: there seems to be a special department of geographical nonsense which is dispensed with airy confidence and usually unchallenged. As an example, I read in the newspaper yesterday – a usually reliable broadsheet – a review of a book about a young official of the Indian Civil Service who had arrived in India in the 1930s and had been given charge of a district 'the size of France'. This is the sort of thing one reads about the days of Empire and it is a nonsense. Even if he had been in charge of the whole of the Punjab – which he wouldn't have been – it would only have been one-third the size of France. People are only too ready to believe these things. For this reason I preserved the letter from the London meteorological office, giving precise information about our hurricane which had been collated from ships in the area. It is so easy for gales to become hurricanes in retrospect.

* * * * *

Our course to Colon took us close to the coast of Colombia, at the point where the peninsula of the province of Guajira sticks out into the Caribbean. It was a most forbidding coast, with no sign of habitation for mile after mile. A place of desolation, so far as I could see; Jim told me that, if we were wrecked there, that would be the end of us. Even if we got ashore, he said 'the natives would eat us'. The thought of striking on such a shore induced in me, at any rate, a strong frisson of alarm and fear. It is what I think of as the 'Diego Ramirez factor'. Off the coast of Tierra del Fuego, near Cape Horn, there is a group of savage rocks, the isles of Diego Ramirez, uninhabitable and awful to behold, known to the British sailors of the time as 'the Dig in the Ribs'. Many ships have wrecked on them and many poor sailors drowned. The set of the southern ocean is directly onto this gruesome little outpost of Chile, and heaven help any sailing ship which found the Diego Ramirez under her lee. A passage in Shalimar's *A Windjammer's Half-Deck* which describes just such an encounter has lodged in my memory like some horrid dream. The four-masted barque *Culrain*, attempting to round Cape Horn on passage to the Chilean coast, is beating to the west against continual headwinds, and her master has underestimated her drift to the east. In the middle of a night of full moon her lookout calls out that he sees a sail on the port bow. The crew are excited – they haven't seen another vessel for more than a month. But the lookout is mistaken; it is not a sail but breakers that he has seen. He calls out again:

> *'Breakers on the lee bow!' A stunning correction! At the same moment Mr. Stanley [the mate], also staring through his glasses, sees a grim pile of rocks standing out of a great cloud of spray. The* Culrain, *driving to the north, must have passed well clear of them; then, sagging to the eastward while wearing round, has brought them into view — perilously close and on a most dangerous bearing. 'My God! The Diego Ramirez!' the mate cried.*

I won't tell you what happened to the *Culrain* after that — this is *Aberdeen Anzac's* story after all — but even as I write this, reflecting that at this very moment the Diego Ramirez are boiling and roaring down there at the bottom of the world, I have a strong sense of the terror that the crew of the *Culrain* must have felt. The Diego Ramirez factor had certainly been operating in my mind the previous winter, off the coast of Galicia.

Besides *Lord Jim* and *Under Western Eyes*, I had brought two other Conrad novels, *Nostromo* and *The Shadow Line*. I read them during the voyage though I confess that I found *Nostromo* heavy going even as I admired it, and skipped through much of it. Apparently, he based his knowledge of Latin America on a very brief visit — hardly more than a glance — to Venezuela in his youth. It is quite extraordinary that he should have been able to do this — but even to ordinary mortals, glimpses are sometimes extremely effective in giving a strong impression of a place. So it was with me as I studied the Guajira peninsula through my binoculars. In Willemstad I had bought a copy of the *South American Handbook*. At that time it was published by the Royal Mail Line and was — still is — a fascinating annual. It was my principal reading matter for several weeks; I devoured it.

I became obsessed by the whole idea of South America, but my favourite area of interest was the Republic of Colombia, and in particular the river boats which used to maintain a regular service on the Magdalena River between Barranquilla and Bogota. The 1960 edition of the handbook makes nostalgic reading. Colombia was a comparatively safe and peaceful place; travellers were not continually warned about muggings, drug searches by police and the other hazards of travel in South America today. The highly recommended steamers, multi-decked vessels with accommodation in four classes and large stocks of cold Barranquilla beer, moved up and down the river through jungle full of monkeys, with lightning flickering in rainy skies. I longed to make the trip but never did and now it is too late: there is no mention of those steamers in the 2000 edition.

I have to admit that after reading of the delights of travel in Colombia in the *Handbook*, my study of the coast through binoculars was disappointing. Like many of my generation, my mental picture of various parts of the world, as yet unseen, had been formed by reading in childhood. Snippets of novels, poems, even hymns, had lodged in the growing mind. 'Greenland's icy mountain, India's coral strand': if you sing that often enough, that is the image you will have of Greenland and India. These images can be so powerful that they can overbear the evidence of your eyes. I know perfectly well that the Danube is not blue, yet at the same time I feel that it is. My notions of the tropics were formed by a line from John Masefield's 'Cargoes', learnt by heart at school:

> *Stately Spanish galleon coming from the Isthmus,*
> *Dipping through the tropics by the palm-green shores.*

I took it that this could only mean the Isthmus of Panama, that Masefield's galleon was on her way back to Spain from Nombre de Dios. So, quite wrongly, I assumed that she would have 'dipped' along the coast of the Guajira peninsula, and that their shores would be palm-green. They were certainly not – they were forbiddingly brown and rocky. But when I look at an historical map of New Granada, I see that the galleon would not have sailed in that direction at all, but probably via Cuba, so the palm green shores would have been the coast of Nicaragua or of Cuba itself.

It was during our passage to Colon that I became aware of the problem of AA's leak. The engineers had already been concerned about it for several days. The general consensus was that the sea was getting in through a collection of small leaks through the caulking, or a bigger one through the stern gland, or the rudder trunking, or all three. But what was very clear was the need for regular pumping out – either mechanically or by Dave having his daily workout with the deck pump. We discussed what we should do. We could not afford to have her slipped when we reached the Panama Canal, so we decided that in due course, when the opportunity presented itself, we would beach her to examine her bottom, harden up the caulking in her seams, and see if we could discover the cause. In the conventional type of carvel-constructed wooden boat this can be a mysterious problem. She might, for example, have spewed some of her caulking, but there was no means of finding that out while she was afloat. Sometimes the older type of racing yachts leaked mightily when going to windward, because the pull of the main shrouds tended to tug open the planking on the weather side. We knew that this could not have been the case with AA because her rig was too stumpy to provide that sort of leverage on her shrouds. The engineers thought it was most probable that the leak was coming in through the stern gland and they knew that we would have to do something about it before we started off across the Pacific.

Our progress towards Colon was made much more

comfortable by the extra fuel we had taken on board, in drums, at Willemstad. Six drums lashed against the bulwarks on each side, each drum containing forty gallons of fuel, had the effect of slowing our roll from a quick lurch, with a jerk at the end, to a stately motion altogether more dignified and agreeable. Life in the galley was much improved, as was any presence in the wheelhouse, because the motion increases as you get higher up in a ship.

This improvement reminded me of a story by Conrad that I had read at school – it had been part of his memoirs, *The Mirror of the Sea*, a set book for the 1946 School Certificate. Conrad has been so thoroughly worked over and analysed by literary critics that it tends not to be emphasised that he was a practical seaman, with a Master Mariner's certificate, utterly steeped in sea lore and the practicalities of a sailor's life. The outline of the story is that he had been appointed mate of a sailing ship, loading in Amsterdam for Java in the dead of winter. His cargo was delayed by the bitter cold – as Conrad puts it, 'cargoes were frozen up-country in barges and schuyts.' When the thaw came, Conrad's cargo arrived in a rush. His captain has not yet joined, but Conrad loads his ship in accordance with the precepts laid down in the standard work on the subject of cargo stowage, *Stevens on Stowage*. This work, as Conrad explains, 'gives you the official teaching on the whole subject, is precise as to rules, mentions illustrative events, quotes law cases where verdicts turned upon a point of stowage.' As a general rule, Conrad knew that it was customary to stow one-third of the weight above the beams – that is, in the upper part of the cargo space, so that is what he did. But when the captain eventually arrives to take command, he tells Conrad that though customary, that rule does not apply in the case of this ship; and the consequence is that they have a most uncomfortable passage to Java. The centre of gravity is too low:

Neither before or since have I felt a ship roll so abruptly, so violently, so heavily. Once she began, you felt that she would never stop, and this hopeless sensation, characterising the motion of ships whose centre of gravity is brought down too low in loading, made everyone of board weary of keeping on his feet.

Poor Conrad was knocked off his feet by part of a flying spar, and during a stay of three months in hospital in Java he pondered the lesson that no two ships are the same. AA reacted very favourably to having her centre of gravity raised by about 3,000 pounds of extra weight at deck level, but, of course, as we pumped the diesel from the drums one by one into the main tanks, she gradually went back to her old ways; cursing could be heard in the galley again.

But that was all in the future; our passage to Colon was blissfully sedate. On May 8th we entered the Caribbean locks, to lie alongside until a pilot was appointed to take us through. An agreeable fellow, he thought we were something of a joke and a welcome diversion from his normal duties. I cannot say that the passage of the canal was a happy experience. It rained very heavily for most of the time, such a downpour that our visibility was much reduced. We went through in company with what seemed a huge Japanese freighter, the *Something Maru*, tucked under her stern frighteningly close to her huge threshing propeller (she must have been in ballast) with her great elliptical stern looming above our bow. At one point a couple of us jumped up onto the canal side to be promptly chased back on board by aggressive canal police. Nothing is just 'not allowed' in the Canal Zone: it is 'very strictly forbidden'. The heat was exhausting, 105 degrees in the galley and 110 degrees in the engine room. Our deck ought to have been a 'hard hat' area (but wasn't), on account of the large, hard 'monkey's fists' which were hurled down by the lock workers – they could have knocked you senseless if you had got in the way. Canal rules dictated that AA maintain a minimum speed of seven knots, in effect our maximum. This strain resulted in an ominous new noise which we began to notice about halfway to Balboa. It came from the engine room: a loud phhht-phhht-phhht, quickly diagnosed as a blown gasket. This sound was accentuated by the echo as we passed through the Gaillard Cut; Dick was stony-faced.

Having read in the *Handbook* that monkeys lurked in the trees on the islands of Gatun lake, I used the few breaks in the downpour to search for them with my binoculars, but saw nothing. There was, I admit, a beauty about the place, but it was overlaid with an atmosphere of brooding sadness as if the ghosts of the twenty thousand workers who had died building the canal lingered in the air. We were depressed at the thought of the sweaty struggle that faced our engineers in dealing with the blown gasket, quite apart from the problem of the leak or leaks – another sweaty struggle which we knew could not be avoided, with no guarantee of success in either case. Nevertheless we moored alongside in Balboa with a sense of achievement, not so much on account of having put the canal behind us as of having entered the Pacific. This gave Nigel particular satisfaction and he wrote to Jean that 'this is the same ocean that washes up on the beach at Woodgate – or Black Island which you love so well.'

One benefit from the canal had been ample hot fresh water collected by bucket from under the outlet of the engine cooling discharge pipe, so we were reasonably clean, shaved and presentable when we went into Panama City by bus. I went with Bill; he was often my companion on these rubbernecking expeditions because he shared my curiosity and inquisitiveness. His readiness to investigate strange places, with his characteristic wondering air, had involved him in real and imagined adventures: it was Bill who had his ears pulled by the ape in Gibraltar, and who had seen the spilt blood in the Tangier kasbah.

As we crossed the border from the Canal Zone into the Republic of Panama, I knew that I was being reminded of something, of somewhere else that I couldn't quite place. It came to me as we returned over the same road: it was the same in 1952 when I had driven across the border from Northern Ireland to Eire: the need to slow down because of the potholes. We left our bus at a large dusty municipal park containing a few busts of nineteenth-century Panamanian heroes on their plinths, dotted about among the sad shrubs. Anxious not to miss anything, I looked at a few of these memorials, but didn't recognise the names, until Bill pulled me away to go and have a drink in a large noisy bar. From there, in order to escape the heat and humidity, we walked to the great Hilton Hotel which we knew would be air-conditioned – a valuable treat – and where we paid a dollar each for Coca-Colas. As it was not proving to be a very interesting outing, we started back to the bus stop; we reckoned we'd 'done' Panama City. On the way we passed some angry women sitting on the bonnets of parked cars. They shouted at us, 'Get out!' 'Americans go home!' They were enraged, apparently, because of some dispute over the Panamanian right to have their national flag flown in the Canal Zone. Bill whistled at them and told them they were beautiful, so they shouted some more abuse, at which we quickly got on the bus, not wanting to be mistakenly attacked for being Americans.

This little episode proved to be the only antagonism we encountered in Panama; nor had there been any warnings about muggings. Looking back on 1960 it seems to have been a pretty crime-free year. We bought some stores from a Panama City wholesaler and he treated us very fairly, indeed generously. I noticed that his forefinger had a pink blotch on it, then noticed that everybody had a similar blotch on their fingers too, so I asked him what it meant. He explained that there had been an election and that this was a crude but effective way to ensure that nobody voted twice. This simple device must have cut out a lot of paperwork.

The most important job in Panama fell to Les, and it put his powers of negotiation very severely to the test. He went to see the Ecuadorian consul about a visa for the Galapagos. We already knew that this matter of a visa was going to be difficult. William Albert Robinson had described in his *Deep Water and Shoal* the somewhat high-handed way in which he had managed to avoid paying anything at all, after being told in the first place that it would cost $60 – a large sum in 1928. Being of a steely disposition, he remonstrated. The charge was promptly halved to $30, the explanation for the $60 being that he had arrived a few minutes late at the consul's office, necessitating a double charge on account of the inconvenience. Robinson felt that $30 was still far too much so he resorted to gringo clout. He made an appointment to see the Minister of the Ecuadorian Legation, who wrote to his friend Don Victor Naranjo, the Governor of the Galapagos, with the result that no charge at all was levied. I wondered about this, but Les and I concluded that if we tried a similar dodge it would probably backfire; the old-boy network used by Robinson would not have served us at all. Another small boat voyager, Sidney Howard, wrote about his passage from Panama to the Marquesas in 1932 in his book *Thames to Tahiti*. I referred to it much later, curious to see how he had managed the visa problem. He tried to land on the islands and had a nasty time of it because of weather conditions but he makes no mention of a visa so I suppose he never attempted to get one. Eric Hiscock in *Wanderer III* didn't try, knowing the difficulties and the risks involved in landing without one. He just pushed straight on for the Marquesas.

We were all determined that we would visit the

Galapagos, come what may. To pass them by would be unthinkable. Les came back from the consulate in gloom. In spite of his best efforts, dressed in full captain's kit, white shirt and shorts, with braided cap at a jaunty angle, charged with a full Australian repertoire of quips, anecdotes and charm, he had been unable to shift the consul. Each of the twelve of us would have to pay, to the best of my recollection, at least $150 – far too much. But Les was not defeated. From a word he had with the British consul the idea emerged that if we were to break down when near the Galapagos, a likely event given AA's reputation, we could take shelter in order to carry out essential repairs. The Governor would probably be reasonable about an emergency of that nature – indeed it was required of him that he should be. This was not advice, naturally; just an observation which might not have occurred to us. We thought it very likely that we would break down near the islands.

We had a most disagreeable task to undertake before we left Panama: dealing with our leak. We found a place on the other side of the harbour from Balboa where we could prop AA against a derelict barge and work on her while the tide was out. We spent three awful days in this dreary spot, lying, for the most part, under her hull in muddy puddles, surrounded by inquisitive crabs, while we hardened up her caulking, putting a coat of antifouling on top for good measure. Every afternoon at three o'clock precisely, there would be a thunderstorm and a downpour of rain. The crabs would advance. The mosquitoes were voracious and too big. The pelicans were the only respectable creatures: in the unhurried, benevolent way they moved about, they made up for the unpleasant screechings, hummings and croaks which surrounded us. Bright eyes could be seen in the jungle; the place seethed with wildlife. To give AA a list towards the barge we had to move all the oil drums, then move them back again. As the tide left her AA sat down too far from the barge, so that she lay over at angle of 40 degrees. For Pam and Muriel, life in the galley was insupportable. It was all a nightmare. As for the leak, whether it was in the rudder trunking, or coming in through the keel bolts, we had done what we could and moved back into our berth at Balboa with great relief.

The next day, the day before we sailed for the Galapagos, I was sitting on deck talking to a Zone policeman. For some reason nobody else was about, just the two of us. Suddenly he staggered and nearly fell over. He righted himself and told me that the reason for his impromptu little dance was that there had been a small earthquake. AA, cushioned in the water, had hardly moved, but on land he'd felt the force of it. Once again I had the sense of a pursuing nemesis, that it was time we left Balboa. There was no pleasure in visiting Panama City again. Castro was stirring up more trouble there, the Stars and Stripes were being burnt regularly in the main square, with effigies of Uncle Sam – the usual forms of protest open to the helpless. We sailed on May 13th.

* * * * *

The Gulf of Panama, into which we motored, is a frustrating place, notorious for fickle winds, or no wind. In the days of sail ships would often spend weary weeks attempting to reach the Pacific trade-wind area. The surface of the water has strange smooth patches, and is often marked by great whirling disturbances, for no apparent reason. But, of course, there is a reason: the Humboldt Current, which flows up the west coast of South America and meets a counter-current in the Gulf. The Pilot Book is not encouraging (it hardly ever is) and, as W. A. Robinson quotes from it in *Deep Water and Shoal*: 'The navigation in this region becomes one of the most tedious, uncertain, and vexatious undertakings known to the seaman.' Under power of course we could ignore these ancient challenges, and we progressed at about five knots with a mysteriously reduced phhht-phhht-phhht coming from the engine room. We had, I think, become used to our blown gasket. We had decided not to deal with it – yet. Perhaps we thought to keep it as an excuse for stopping at the Galapagos.

As always, as soon as we had left the land behind us, we seemed to become the only ship in the world, moving through this strange and mildly sinister gulf. The emptiness of the oceans of the world always struck me. I can recall seeing only one ship during our entire time crossing the Atlantic and Pacific. Where had all the ships we had seen going through the Canal disappeared to? One of them, headed for the Caribbean, had been the French Messageries Maritimes liner, the *Mélanésien*. I had stared into her first-class accommodation as she moved slowly past, seeing the comfortable, indeed luxurious arrangements made for her fortunate passengers, and I rather wished that I could change places, for a couple of days at any rate, with one of them. I have never been a liner passenger but have always longed to be, and now it is too late – cruise ships are not at all the same thing. The shipping companies' advertisements which I pored over on the front page of *The Times* of those days called up wonderful voyages in the lap of luxury dressing for dinner on the *Rangitani*, for example, or cocktails on the boat deck of the *Southern Cross*. I was an expert in ocean voyaging without ever actually buying a ticket. Nor did I spurn the humbler passenger cargo boats, having a particular affection for the Ellerman Line steamers, *City of This and That*. Some of them would do very nicely for carrying me around the world, possibly better than a large passenger liner, more intimate and friendly, but the food just as good. My favourite was the New Zealand Shipping Company, though I had never actually seen any of their ships. Their names sounded like heaven to me – *Rangitoto, Rangitani, Rangitiki, Ruahine* – these names had stolen my wits away just as Chimborazo and Cotopaxi had stolen the poet Turner's soul away. There is a great power of suggestion in names – no one with any imagination can be indifferent to the coast of Coromandel, where the early pumpkins blow. It was largely because of ships' names that I had become the world's leading expert on ocean travel.

Anyway, we didn't see any ships, but we did see something interesting when I was at the wheel early one morning. It was a baulk of timber about 30 feet long, covered in a thick blanket of weed, floating in the water. By the length and density of the weed I judged that it had been in the water for many months, possibly years, slowly circulating with the ocean currents. It looked innocent enough, bobbing in the sunlight, but if a wooden yacht at speed had struck it end on, it could have stove in her planking. For a moment I thought we should take it in tow, but then thought to hell with it. I am reminded of one of Shalimar's best and most frightening stories, *Beatrice Lee: Derelict.* The Yankee clipper *Beatrice Lee*, built in Massachusetts in the 1870s, after a career of several decades, becomes a floating derelict and a menace to shipping. She slowly circulates round the Atlantic, a weed-covered black hump in the water, until she is struck in the night by the fine steamship *Blantyre* on passage from Halifax to Glasgow. The *Blantyre* founders with all hands save the third mate. As Shalimar tells this tale, it is a horror story, and if I had remembered it in the Gulf I would have taken that weed-covered baulk of timber in tow for the Galapagos.

During the week that we took to get there Jim and I had ongoing discussions on geographical–meteorological matters, often conducted on deck beside the hatchway to our cabin, in the eyes of the ship: a good place to observe the antics of the dolphins. I didn't understand then, and am still uncertain, why the water level on the Pacific side of the Panama Canal is 20 centimetres or 8 inches higher than that on the Caribbean side. I taxed Jim with this strange fact, pointing out that water is supposed to find its own level. He thought that as it is many thousands of miles round South America and back up to the Caribbean, it was reasonable to assume that there would be a difference. I said that the canal had been completed in 1914, the water had had 46 years to find its level, so how long did it want? There the discussion stalled; I still have no answer, but I surmise that it has to do with prevailing winds and ocean drift.

By this time, mid May, we were about six months into our adventure. We were an odd-looking ship's company. Jim, Bill, Dave and John had shaved their heads; Nigel had grown a fine beard which gave him a patriarchal appearance though he was only 33. The brave girls were hardly fashionable. As for me, most of my clothes had been stolen in Corunna or Barbados and I was reduced to jeans, white cotton shirts and one red shirt that no thief had wanted. Dick had a respectable beard which suited him well. Nigel and John both had wives ashore; all four of them were friends. John was a steady correspondent and kept his wife, Phyll, informed about our movements and plans. Nigel wrote long letters but erratically. He had received a letter from Jean when we were in Panama, pointing out that whereas she, Jean, was in the dark, Phyll was up to date on AA's news. Nigel was not pleased with John for this treachery. He went about the ship for a time muttering (he was a good mutterer), 'John had time to write; oh yes, John had time to tell *his* wife where he was.' John was meant to feel bad about this perceived lack of mate's solidarity, but it struck me that he continued insouciant.

I think we had an easy time of it in the Gulf of Panama compared with other voyagers. Nobody has ever had a good word for this part of the ocean. The three yachtsmen I have mentioned all had a horrible struggle with contrary winds, and rainstorms. We never bothered to try to sail, but just chuntered along at about five knots. Pam and Muriel tried to vary our diet, which had become too dependent on tinned pork and rice, plus dorado as caught. We all wondered what fresh food we would find in the Galapagos. Dave suggested the possibility of turtle soup – out of the question as the turtles are protected. Nobody showed any interest in eating iguanas. Dave, a keen amateur evolutionist, had many theories about flying fish, birds, penguins and other creatures, which he would expound to anyone who would listen. We hoped he would at least find food for thought when we reached Chatham Island. George was intent on cold beer, preferably the Barranquilla brew which had improved his life since Willemstad, and I longed for good coffee; possibly it was grown on the island? All these hopes, and we did not even know whether we would be allowed to land. It was at this time that the hammerhead shark was landed on the afterdeck, a very gory business, and that Nigel nearly caught his great sea monster. The dolphins were an entirely different matter, as I have no doubt they feel themselves to be. From time to time they would come racing across the sea like a pack of hounds, to gambol around our bows.

Of all our crew Dick was the most energetic and restless. Being responsible for the engine should have been enough for him, but he became interested in sailing as well. In our earlier sailing days in the Atlantic I would sometimes see him on deck at night, taking a pull on the sheets here and there, studying the effects of small adjustments. He was very strong: sometimes when I was struggling with some heavy job like hoisting the gaff, he turned up silently to help me.

I put in some time, as we motored to the Galapagos, repairing sails, with a sailmaker's palm, often engaged in desultory conversation with George. The pleasure of handling flax sails and manilla bolt-rope is one which must now be almost entirely lost. The sail cloth is soft and flexible, the fat rope's strands easy to open to push the sailmaker's needle through. It is a peaceful occupation; it also has the virtue of being a job which can take as long as you want it to. No one would wonder why I was spending a whole day on one sail – the work had that slight element of mystery which kept critics at bay – though there was one disturbing moment when Nigel came to watch me for a few minutes, then got up and moved away saying, 'That doesn't look too difficult.' He himself had made a beautiful wooden fife rail which had been very difficult, so he was in a strong position to monitor other people's activities. I continued to make porridge for breakfast, doling it out into bowls on the galley table in carefully equal portions. Then I would open the galley door and shout 'All the same size!' at which Bill, Gannet Bill, always the first to appear and with lightning glance, would seize the largest portion, because of course they never were exactly equal. I admired his split-second selection, with no dithering.

I would talk with Nigel as he sat in his improvised

shelter in the stern, and I found out quite a lot about Australia – the old Australia that has probably been heavily diluted by now. I asked him what his friends in Queensland would say when he told them of how he travelled back from England. 'They'll say, *Jeezus, yousl've been a long time then.*' I cannot possibly reproduce the manner and accent of this remark.

In the approach to Chatham Island the Humboldt Current was evidently dominant, for the air became cooler even as we crossed the equator; George complained that he hadn't come all that way to sit on deck in his sweater. Nearing Wreck Bay, the entry port, I studied the island as it gradually appeared, uninviting, from a grey mist. It had a slightly encouraging greenish tinge, but it was nobody's idea of a tropical island. A shanty town straggled along the rim of the bay, with a rickety pier as its focal point and behind it a solid-looking building on which flew a large Ecuadorian flag. I spotted a church and a few other larger structures, but the whole had a depressing air. We dragged our 112 lb plough anchor forward and hung it over the bow while we circled slowly, deciding where to drop it. We settled on a berth near the end of the jetty, and as our cable ran out a motor launch approached at speed, the Ecuadorian flag at the stern, containing a naval officer together with four sailors armed with rifles. Trouble.

The arrival of an ensign (the equivalent of a sub-lieutenant in the Royal Navy) with his armed bluejackets was from a practical point of view an advantage, in that our visit would now be regularised, even if we were immediately sent off with a flea in our ear. In *Around the World in Wanderer III*, Eric Hiscock had accurately pointed out that landing on the Galapagos without permission could have horrible consequences: 'An Ecuadorian gunboat frequently visited the group, and it was not unknown for fishing boats and even yachts whose papers were not in order to be seized and their crews taken off to Ecuador.'

We were taking a risk which I do not think any of us would take today. In 1960 there was a residual assumption of British invulnerability and exemption from the usual restrictions of travel in the less sophisticated parts of the world. There was the unspoken – or indeed spoken – thought that we could surely talk our way out of any trouble posed by Ecuador; a thought fully shared by the Australians, especially Les. As the boarding party clambered over the side, he appeared in his captain's hat and went to work on the sulky young ensign with his full battery of antipodean charm. The plan was to explain to the authorities that we had engine trouble and wanted to lie in Wreck Bay for a few days while carrying out essential repairs. There was no difficulty in demonstrating the truth of our claims: apart from the blown gasket, we had intermittent non-functioning of the water pump which Dick fully intended to deal with. Les, Dick and the ensign disappeared into the engine room, while the bluejackets lounged on deck, trailing their rifles. They sat on the bulwarks smoking cigarettes and accepted gratefully Muriel's offered cup of tea. Their rifles, which looked like ex-British Army Lee Enfields left over from the war, vaguely reassured me. They gave the group a homely appearance. While the engine party was gone, we tried to look busy, coiling down lines and tidying the deck. Tim tried Spanish conversation with the bluejackets, without success. We all tried to look like honest sailors who had suffered misfortune. After twenty minutes Les and Dick and the ensign reappeared; it was impossible to read from their faces any indication of what our fate would be, but Les and the ensign, together with two of the bluejackets, climbed back into the launch and roared away back to the jetty. Les's face was a mask. Nigel muttered, 'If they put him in jail, we'd better get out of here quick.'

Two hours passed; the remaining bluejackets consumed more tea. We studied Wreck Bay through binoculars, aware that this was likely to be the nearest we were destined to approach it, but there wasn't much to see. Then the launch came back with Les and the ensign in it. Jim said, 'I don't think he's under arrest.' All the Ecuadorians then went away and we heard what had happened. Les had been taken to see the Commandante, a commander in the Ecuadorian navy, who was also the Governor of the Galapagos and who was most agreeable and understanding. They had had a drink together, swapping stories. This amicable get-together produced permission for us to stay for a few days, but we must be gone before the Admiral came over from Guayaquil in a destroyer, in about a week's time, on an inspection tour. The Commandante didn't want the Admiral to see us, for obvious reasons. It was also to be clearly understood that when we left we really left, not calling at any other island in the group. Les thought the Commandante had not believed our story, but assumed that we would behave well and not cause him any trouble. If we did, he implied, we would be sorry.

* * * * *

According to William Robinson, the Galapagos were discovered by the Bishop of Panama, Berlanga, in 1535, apparently by accident, his ship having been carried into the archipelago by currents during a period of prolonged calm. It must have been very frightening – the Spanish sailors were probably glad they had a bishop on board. They would have had no idea what was going to happen to them next, as their ship was carried helplessly among those weird islands at the very edge of the world. Wreck Bay was a primitive place when Robinson was there in 1928, and it had not developed much by 1960. Having landed our dinghy at the jetty we saw that the town, if it could be called such, lay along the curve of the bay and petered out about 100 yards inland. The buildings reminded me of photographs I had seen of 'townships' in the Australian outback; ramshackle buildings of two stories, with deep verandas on the first floor. As we walked along the cindery road which ran along the sea front, we passed a group of what I imagine were the island's leading citizens, sitting on one of these verandas, a mafia-like bunch in dark glasses who watched us silently. I thought of the malevolent baddies sitting outside the saloon bar in *Shane* – in fact, I think I saw Jack Pallance among them.

I was looking for a post office, as I had written cards to friends in England who I hoped would be impressed by the Galapagos stamps. I found it, a large room in what was also the telegraph office, where two young women took my money promising to stamp and send the cards. I went away thinking they would never be posted but in fact they all reached their destinations so my suspicions were quite unfounded. Chatham Island had been for many years a prison colony, with many prisoners still resident, and it did seem like just the sort of place where we would be cheated, but nothing disagreeable happened to us during our visit. Further along the road, a woman invited us to see a giant tortoise. Sure enough, there was the enormous beast in a shed behind her house, with a donkey for company. I stared at the tortoise, wondering if Charles Darwin had met him during his visit in 1836. I have recently read of a tortoise called Pepe, in the 2000 edition of the *South American Handbook*, who might be the same creature. Whoever he was, he wasn't doing much, nor was his friend the donkey. Giant tortoises live to a great age – apparently to over 300 years in some cases, so it must be supposed that they need to conserve their energies, resisting the temptation to indulge in pointless display for the benefit of tourists.

Forty years after the voyage of the *Aberdeen Anzac*, I read Darwin's *Voyage of the Beagle*; I wish that I had read it sooner. It is full of interest and written in the limpid economical manner that was typical of the best writing of the time. Never do his scientific preoccupations become boring to the non-scientific – i.e. me. He spent much time ashore, and records that:

> *As I was walking along I met two large tortoises, each of which must have weighed at least two hundred pounds; one was eating a piece of cactus, and as I approached, it stared at me and slowly stalked away; the other gave a deep hiss, and drew in its head. These huge reptiles, surrounded by the black lava, the leafless shrubs and large cacti, seemed to my fancy like some antediluvian animals. The few dull-coloured birds cared no more for me than they did for the great tortoises.*

During his stay on Chatham Island he often rode on the backs of tortoises, of which there were a great number in his day: 'I frequently got on their backs, and then giving a few raps on the hinder part of their shells, they would rise up and walk away; – but I found it very difficult to keep my balance.' Reading this I had a mental picture of the 'Old Person of Ickley, who could not abide to ride quickly; He rode to Karnak, on a Tortoise's back, That moony Old Person of Ickley.' I searched through my copy of Edward Lear's *Book of Nonsense* and, sure enough, there he was, the

Old Person of Ickley, drawn by Lear, wearing what looks like a round sailor's hat, holding a whip, sitting insecurely on the back of a cross-looking tortoise. This was first published in the 1840s (it is, to be precise, in the book of *More Nonsense*), shortly after the publication of *The Voyage of the Beagle*, and I surmise that Darwin's work inspired Lear to create the moony Old Person. Wherever Ickley is – and does it exist? – my mind now connects it firmly with the Galapagos Islands.

The iguana was another of Darwin's particular interests and I think he treated these reptiles abominably, even allowing for the different attitude towards the natural world in his day. He experimented on them mercilessly, presumably always in the spirit of research. He 'opened' them to see what they had just eaten, and he threw them about like soft toys. He described them as 'hideous looking creatures, of dirty black colour, stupid, and sluggish in its movements.' One wretched iguana of the marine species, *Amblyrhynchus cristatus*, was thrown repeatedly by its tail into a deep pool to see if it would swim back to where Darwin stood after throwing it. It always did, no doubt unable to believe that he would throw it in yet again. As Darwin surmises, he was the very first enemy that the reptile had ever encountered on land, and, being stupid, it couldn't conceive of such a thing as a land-based threat. Turning to the terrestrial species he bullies one in a different way, waiting until it has half buried itself in its burrow, then pulling it by the tail:

> *I watched on for a long time, till half its body was buried; then I walked up and pulled it by the tail; at this it was greatly astonished, and soon shuffled up to see what was the matter; and then stared at me in the face, as much as to say, 'What made you pull my tail?'*

What indeed? Darwin and the iguanas remind me of God and poor Job as recounted in the *Book of Job*. Just as God torments Job to see how much he will endure, so Darwin harries the iguana to discover its reactions. But at least Job didn't have his stomach 'opened'.

The Galapagos Islands are mostly basalt, being the peaks of old volcanos. The rather gloomy foreshore of blackish rocks and greyish sand was enlivened while we were there by the locals bathing in the cold water, with much cheerful shrieking, and many good-natured dogs running about. On our second day I explored Wreck Bay more thoroughly, starting with a visit to the church to see what it could tell me. It was a plain building, with little decoration either inside or out, save the Stations of the Cross in simple aquatint, but a peaceful and welcoming atmosphere. There was certainly no suggestion of money to spare on Chatham Island.

Having inspected his church I went in search of the priest, whom I had seen on the jetty when I came ashore, a round-faced young man with spectacles. He was in his fishing dinghy having trouble with the outboard motor that wouldn't start. He was wearing a brown coat with the words 'All Wool' on the back. I think he had put it on inside out. I called down to advise him to leave the outboard for a few minutes. Shouting advice to people in boats is normally a dreadful thing to do – but I went on to explain that in my experience of outboards, if they don't start after a few pulls on the cord, the carburettor is probably flooded, so it's best to leave them alone for a while. He grinned and sat down. His English was not quite good enough for conversation so we just sat there for about five minutes in silence. I would have liked to ask him about his attendance figures; whether he liked his life in Wreck Bay or would he prefer another posting, but even if he had been able to understand, my questions would have been too brash. I wondered about the life of a young priest in such a place, but assumed that if he was a good priest it wouldn't make any difference to him where he was. Then he wound the cord round the starter again, pulled hard, and the engine burst into life. Off he went to his fishing with a cheerful wave. A memorable encounter.

That evening Bill, Tim and I had dinner at Mama's Restaurant on the beach. It was a simple square structure made of breezeblocks up to three feet high, with posts holding up a roof. In a corner of the square, separated by more breezeblocks, was the kitchen where Mama presided. She was a large Ecuadorian, I believe from Guayaquil, and her handsome and intelligent son of about twenty helped her in the enterprise. She was a wonderful cook; we ate a splendid steak dinner, drinking aguardiente followed by Barranquilla beer. The son confided that he would like to get away from Chatham Island – wanted to be a motor mechanic in Guayaquil, see some life and have some future – but didn't want to leave Mama. Later, I talked to Mama. She said that she wanted her son to get to Ecuador where he could see some life and have a future, but that he felt he should stay with her. A bit of an impasse and possibly a lack of communication; I told the son he ought to go and I didn't think his mother would mind. I hope he went. At dinner we were joined by an American from an 'experiment in living' group based in the old derelict factory. His greatest interest was motor cycling (which he pronounced 'sickling'); I had not seen a single motor cycle on Chatham Island, although it would have been a good place for scrambling. He would have been much happier if he had had his machine to ride around on, but he really wanted to go back to Minnesota. It was clear that the 'experiment' was not working out, and this seems to have been a characteristic of the Galapagos.

The next morning the regular steamer from Guayaquil arrived, a dreadful old tub, streaked with rust. By comparison with her, for the first time since leaving England we were the smartest boat in the harbour, for a few hours. The steamer brought supplies and would take away whatever the island produced – coffee, bananas, sugar cane, maybe some of the unsweet and unjuicy oranges. These oranges Pam and I sampled on a walk we took to Progresso, five miles distant, uphill all the way on a dusty red earth road, becoming muddy as we climbed into the mist. I picked an unsatisfactory one from an orange grove by the road, but higher up Pam tried one that was better.

I wanted to see Progresso because William Robinson had spent some time there during his visit in 1928 in the company of a heroic Norwegian girl, Karin, who farmed land around Progresso. It is a strange and moving story, in which it is easy to detect a romance between Robinson and Karin, short-lived though it must have been – he arrived at Chatham Island on about November 20th and was gone by the morning of December 2nd. There are echoes in it, for me, of the tale of Dido and Aeneas: Karin as Dido, ruling over her tiny estate on horseback, riding among her peons with a pistol in her pocket. Aeneas Robinson has a world to circumnavigate; he has to 'move on'. He makes his brief stay memorable in no more than three pages of his book. Apparently Karin, her father and brother and about eighty Norwegians, had come out to Chatham Island in 1926 to form a farming colony, together with all their possessions – furniture, farming equipment, tractor and wagons. The venture failed, as such ventures often do, through lack of capital. Nearly all of the party drifted away, Karin's father and brother proved unequal to the struggle and she was left to manage everything alone. She ruled with complete authority over her workforce of peons and discharged convicts; they obeyed her without question. Robinson had brought with him aboard his yacht *Svaap* a small brown honey bear, from Panama. The bear had not been happy afloat, so when *Svaap* sailed from Wreck Bay he was left with Karin with whom, Robinson tells us 'he had found a new and happier home'.

The name Progresso appealed to me because I knew that there would be no evidence of progress, and it did not disappoint; it was just as I expected. There was a huge square of bare earth, surrounded by shacks, with some cowboys on horseback grouped in the middle. These were I suppose the local 'vaqueros', more glamorous in the imagination than in the flesh. Having seen Progresso, Pam and I had to get back, preferably without walking. We were lucky: a tractor with a flat cart in tow gave us a lift to Wreck Bay. You may wonder what had happened to Karin and her farm and I am ashamed to admit that I never found out. It had been too long ago, the story had gone cold, the language difficulty defeated me. Now, I am half glad I never knew the end of the tale because the fragment contained in Robinson's book has a completeness of its own, properly ending with his departure, leaving her with the honey bear.

While we were at Wreck Bay, there was an Ecuadorian general election. I have some photographs of the event from which it would appear that more donkeys attended than voters. They are standing all over the place, while the election is carried forward in the open, at trestle tables. This took place over the weekend of June 4th/5th, and I can record that Dr Jose Maria Valasco Ibarra was voted President for the fourth time. He had on earlier occasions been deposed twice, so we can assume that he was a hardy perennial of the Ecuadorian political scene, with great staying, or rather coming-back, power.

Well aware that we were at Chatham Island on sufferance, we knew we had to leave soon. The Commandante could see us every day from the balcony of his Residence; we were sure that we were an irritant. The destroyer from Guayaquil with the Admiral on board might arrive any day and quite likely the Commandante himself did not know quite when. It is, after all, the sort of thing a British Admiral would do: turn up unexpectedly. So we arranged a farewell banquet on the beach, involving Mama, her son, one or two others who seem to have become attached, and the usual gang of dogs who, as we had noticed in Spain, enjoyed great indulgence. Pam and Muriel cooked the easier parts of a pig we'd bought, while Mama cooked the rest with side dishes of fish, rice, breadfruit and I'm not sure what else. I'm a bit dim about this feast which I am assured was memorable.

Our last task before leaving was to buy some food. Because they were cheap, and to add variety to our limited diet, we bought many bananas. We hung the bright green bunches from the fixed awning structures beside the wheelhouse, where they swayed in unison to AA's roll. We hoped the two sacks of violet-coloured potatoes wouldn't sprout before we had eaten them all. No oranges, but some coffee, completed our shopping.

Chatham Island had treated us very fairly but we were not sorry to be leaving it. It had a spirit of mild hopelessness hanging over it. Being a penal colony for many years until 1960 had left a crushed, depressing atmosphere. Referring to my notes, I find that we sailed on May 23rd. That is odd because *The Times* records that the election took place on June 4th/5th, and *The Times* is not wrong, not in 1960. I can only assume that what we witnessed at Wreck Bay, of which I have photographs, was some sort of preliminary election, peculiar to the Galapagos. I certainly didn't dream those donkeys, the trestle tables under the tree, the election papers blowing in the wind, or the men in dark glasses sitting menacingly beside the ballot boxes.

Getting the anchor on AA was not a simple matter. We had no windlass in the usual meaning of the word, but wound in our anchor chain on the big drum of the coiler which sat in the middle of the ship, just forward of the wheelhouse. This rather shaky piece of machinery was operated by Dave, who understood its vagaries. In order not to put too great a strain on it (Dave sucked his teeth and shook his head while operating it) we would help it by pulling on the chain by hand as it emerged dripping from the stemhead roller. When the anchor itself arrived at the stemhead, we would lift it and stow it, secured by ties inside the bulwarks as far forward as was practical. Then we would unshackle it from its chain, winding up the loose end onto the coiler drum. All this done, we had time to look to the shore and see Mama and some other people who were waving goodbye to us. It struck me that, apart from Rastus, they were the only people who had actually waved goodbye from any of our ports of call. That some of the inhabitants should seem to regret our departure reinforced our impression of the loneliness and isolation of Chatham Island.

* * * * *

It will not have escaped the notice of the attentive reader that we had not yet dealt with our blown gasket. It had been left deliberately to display as a defect to the Ecuadorian authorities, but why had Dick and the engine room not repaired it while we lay at anchor in Wreck Bay? Was it that we had seemed to manage well enough all the way from Balboa? – I simply don't know. They overhauled the defective water pump, so it is possible that Dick thought they'd done enough; although no one could have believed that we would reach New Zealand without tackling the gasket. We shaped a course to take us south of Albermarle Island, the biggest in the group, leaving Charles Island to port. They were both shrouded in mist and were so forbidding that even if we had been allowed to we would not have wanted to land. Once again we encountered the weird smooth eddying of the sea's surface, but we were happy that the main current was pushing us to the west where we wanted to go. Robinson had an eerie

experience in these very waters a few days after he had left
Chatham Island:

> *We were becalmed out of sight of land. I suddenly noticed*
> *the compass slowly revolving. In a moment it had*
> *described a complete circle, then another, then another.*
> *Looking over the side I saw that we were motionless in*
> *the water. I made sure that I was awake and not*
> *dreaming. Then I looked aloft and beheld a most*
> *amazing sight. The whole heavens were slowly and*
> *majestically revolving on a centre directly overhead. It was*
> *a most disturbing sensation, and there was the queer*
> *feeling in the pit of my stomach that reminded me of the*
> *feeling I had as a boy when I had ridden too long upon a*
> *merry-go-round. I realised now, of course, that we were in*
> *the grip of a tremendous whirlpool, the whole body of*
> *water as far as I could see in the dim light revolving with*
> *us in the centre, much as a railroad turntable revolves*
> *with a locomotive.*

Nothing quite so dramatic as this happened to AA, but
there is no denying that the waters around the Galapagos
are unusually disturbed and unpredictable. The strong
currents meeting and conflicting for mastery must account
for this. Not surprisingly the early Spanish mariners called
them the Enchanted Islands. I had read three accounts by
yachtsmen of trans-Pacific passages: Robinson, Eric
Hiscock (who, as already mentioned, avoided the
Galapagos altogether) and Sidney Howard in his 14-ton
gaff cutter *Pacific Moon* – built on the lines of a Lancashire
nobbie – who describes his adventures in his book *Thames
to Tahiti*. He went with a shipmate, John Johnstone (who I
had met by chance in Dover in 1957). They had endless
engine trouble. In April 1932 they were making for Wreck
Bay hoping to get water, but a failed water pump (that
sounded familiar!) knocked out their engine and the fickle
winds put them at the mercy of the west-bound current,

sweeping them beyond Chatham Island; very soon they were off the south coast of Albemarle with little chance of being able to either sail or motor back to Chatham. They struggled against the current for sixty hours. Sometimes they lost sight of Albemarle altogether. They closed the land, the wind failed, they then heard breakers and thought they were doomed, as indeed they might well have been. John managed to get the engine working again by dismantling and reassembling the water pump, and they wisely decided to use the last of their petrol to get clear of the awful sinister island. Howard writes, 'The whole place seemed as if it had just been coughed up out of the sea and was a nightmare.' Their engine never ran again. At last they were free of the Galapagos, but even their last sight of Blue Mountain on Albemarle was an omen of new trouble: 'Looking back I saw the blunt cone of Blue Mountain outlined for a moment by a vivid flash of lightning, as though the monster was angry at having missed *Pacific Moon*. A little later I heard a strange sound forward, and I found that the bobstay had snapped.'

That's enough of *Pacific Moon*'s difficulties; we had serious ones of our own. We too were moving along the south coast of Albemarle Island, giving it a wide berth, sensing its evil ways, when the phhht-phhht-phhht of our blown gasket became much louder. A new piece of the gasket must have been blown out by the gas compression. This time we had to do something about it immediately, so we stopped the engine and made what sail we could. Albemarle was a long grey hump to the north, stretching into the distance. The set of the current seemed to be due west, which we thought would carry us clear of any danger, but there was little wind so we had no more than bare steerage way. Dick and his engineers addressed the problem of the gasket. There were four of them crowded into the engine room; sitting at the wheel I could hear again the clink of tools and the occasional expletive. Later,

I heard all about it. The great problem was that there was barely room above the cylinder head to lift it – the deck head lay close to the top of the engine. They had to lift the head by fixing sheaves into the deck head and use wire, because rope would have stretched too much to be effective. Nigel fixed the eye bolts to which the sheaves were shackled. When it came to the actual lifting, AA started to roll more heavily than before, out of general cussedness. The cylinder head was very heavy and wanted to swing from side to side. Fortunately, Dick had a spare gasket set so that as soon as the head had been lifted far enough the old broken gasket could be removed and the new one inserted. After about three hours, the cylinder head had been bolted down, the engine restarted and we were on our way again.

It is about 3,200 miles from the Galapagos to the Marquesas: we had a long haul ahead of us and to conserve our fuel we would have to sail at least half the distance. We found that the trade wind was never as strong or as consistent as it had been in the Atlantic and its direction was not ideal for our course, being from the southeast on our port quarter. On some days we ran barely 80 miles. In order to maximise our sail area, I set the most fragile of our mizzens between the mainmast and the wheelhouse, and swung the twin headsail booms to greatest advantage; the big jib aft was also trimmed to be more effective. But what an absurd rig it was in spite of our best efforts! It is a tribute to AA's underwater shape that we were able to get along as well as we did.

We were still leaking, but not enough to be a worry; our ocean routine was re-established. Afternoon tea again – but no biscuits – and in the evening we drank rum and Coca-Cola, or beer. Pam had devised a dorado meal with rice and tinned pineapple that wasn't at all disagreeable. She and Muriel tried hard to vary our diet. Sometimes we could hear them stumbling about the dark food store behind the aft bulkhead of our fo'c'sle, trying to find something interesting to eat. We enjoyed the violet-coloured Galapagos potatoes until they began to sprout in the hot darkness. The bananas festooned around the wheelhouse did what we should have known that bananas always do: they all ripened on the same day, so we were obliged to have a banana orgy so as not to waste them. Pam and Muriel invented, at short notice, every conceivable permutation of banana dish. For a short time, before I used up the last of the porridge, we offered a choice of porridge or corn flakes for breakfast, just like in a hotel.

Jim re-established his navigation class, well-attended as before. Nigel favoured a new star for his evening sight: Rigel Kent, and Tim thought that he felt proprietorial about it because he had mistaken the name for Nigel Kent. George and I reviewed our reading matter. The more ephemeral paperbacks had mostly disappeared over the side but I still had my small, jealously guarded collection of hardbacks. There was only one poetry anthology among them, *The London Book of English Verse*, edited by Herbert Read and Bonamy Dobree, published by Eyre and Spottiswood in 1949. I still have it, worn and salt-stained. It is long enough – 800 pages – to contain most of the best poems, but George didn't want to read it (nor did anyone else). He buried himself in *Bleak House*, the only Dickens on board, and that kept him quiet for a long time, although it never stirred him in the way that George Eliot had.

Apart from on deck, our social centre was the aft cabin, where we could play cards, smoke, talk and lie about. At the aft end of it stood a large steel safe, propped up on a shelf. This cabin had been the scene of a frightening event during the Biscay hurricane. In the middle of the night AA's bows had pitched down into the trough of a stupendous sea and the safe fell forward into the cabin with a great crash. The whole ship shook; for one terrifying moment I thought she had struck because that is what it felt like in the wheelhouse. The relief when I knew what had happened was enormous. Life at sea: who needs it? I think Dave was the decisive factor in lifting the safe back to its place – I took no part in what must have been a brutal struggle.

One morning, just before dawn, I was on watch but not at the wheel; Dick was steering, having nothing to do in the engine room. I was leaning out of the wheelhouse window (it let down on a leather strap like in an old-fashioned railway carriage) sniffing the dawning day – always a delightful time in the tropics. I heard a loud and explosive hissing and saw, not more than one hundred yards away on our port beam, a family of whales keeping a parallel course, spouting as they went. Through my binoculars I could see that they were of varying sizes, ranging from large up to very large. I hoped they were well disposed towards us, though there is no reason why any whale should be well disposed towards any ship. The scene was just as described in Christopher Smart's poem in the London anthology, 'Strong against tide, th'enormous whale, Emerges, as he goes.'

I thought I knew something about whales because I had read *Moby Dick*, and I was sure that we would be in serious trouble if they became annoyed. They were a dignified and impressive group as they heaved themselves half out of the water, blowing out great sprays of mixed air and water. It is not surprising that they have attracted so much attention over the years, with so many mentions in various writings. All the way back to the 104th Psalm: 'so is the great and wide sea also: wherein are things creeping innumerable, both small and great beasts. There go the ships, and there is that Leviathan: whom thou has made to take his pastime therein.'

Like the early writers, I sensed that the whales were playing, also that we were privileged to be witnessing something we would disturb at our peril, in which quite an advanced intelligence was involved. I supposed that the biggest, about the same length as AA, was the paterfamilias. On they went for about twenty minutes, keeping their speed and distance, and then they all suddenly disappeared. I was alarmed – *Moby Dick* again – thinking they might decide to play by coming up underneath us and smash us to pieces like the *Pequod*. There has recently been published the diary of the mate of the whaling ship *Essex*, destroyed by a giant sperm whale in roughly the same place as we encountered our group, about 1,000 miles west of the Galapagos. The mate, Owen Chase, records seeing this huge beast, 85 feet long, weighing, as he estimates, 80 tons, 'distracted with rage and fury'. The great whale charges at the *Essex* twice, leaving Chase haunted by his memory of 'fury and vengeance'. It is believed that this true story, which took place in 1819, inspired Melville's *Moby Dick*. I find it hard to believe in the 85-foot whale, feeling it may have grown a little in Chase's mind. The *Encyclopaedia Britannica* gives the sperm whale a maximum length of about 63 feet. The impression I had that our group was a family was probably mistaken, for they are polygamous, a school of females being typically accompanied by a couple of males.

After they had disappeared there was an uneasy period

of about five minutes before they all suddenly reappeared to starboard, continuing at the same distance as before. 'I wish I could blow like that,' said Dick. I wished that I could interpret what was going on in their whale minds, but I sensed, by this time, that they were friendly and were keeping us company out of pure curiosity. But how did they know we weren't planning to kill them? Maybe – although this is fanciful – the dolphins who attended us so often had passed them some message that we were harmless. Then, when we had grown accustomed to their presence, they disappeared again, this time for good. I am reasonably certain that 'our' whales were sperm whales – they had the characteristic massive heads of the species. Although they were formidable and awe-inspiring, I had none of the dread that I have sometimes felt for large sea creatures; this may be because, being mammals, one had more of a fellow feeling for them, as one has for dolphins. There is something of horror in the thought of the great deep-sea creatures that lurk far down on the ocean bed, such as the probably mythical Kraken which is so chillingly described by Tennyson in his poem 'The Kraken':

> *Below the thunders of the upper deep;*
> *Far far beneath in the abysmal sea,*
> *His ancient, dreamless, uninvaded sleep*
> *The Kraken sleepeth ...*

Was the Kraken a giant squid? And what atavism inspires fear and loathing of what may well be an imaginary creature? Anyway, whales did not give us the same feeling at all.

After the excitement of the whales, life became uneventful. I found time to be annoyed with George, who was reading the *Dr. Thorne* that I had found in the Vigo bookshop. He was a slow reader and I didn't want to wait nor did I want to have a preview of the plot filtered through his comments. As our deck cargo of diesel fuel was gradually transferred to the main tanks, AA began to roll more quickly, but by this time we had become accustomed to this particular discomfort. Nor did Muriel complain any longer about 'playing with the sails'. Both she and Pam were remarkably uncomplaining – nothing seemed to disconcert or annoy them. Many more grumbles were heard from us chaps. We made our slow way across the Pacific by a mixture of power and sail, sometimes motor-sailing, sometimes sail alone, sometimes power alone, depending on the wind conditions. Tim had prepared a chart showing fuel consumption, working out that we burnt an average of 3½ gallons per hour, when we were under power alone. This, together with the daily measuring of our remaining fuel, enabled us to keep a check on our capacity to motor, bearing in mind that we would not be able to buy more diesel until we reached Tahiti.

One day when our speed had fallen to no more than two knots, some of the crew decided to be dragged along in the sea for a 'swim'. With lines round them, they were lowered over the side, one by one. It was surprising how, even at such a low speed, they made such a great disturbance in the water. A bird followed us for some distance, very high in the sky behind; it must have been an albatross. It never came to inspect us, nor did it alter its position. It just stayed up there, looking to right and left, hardly moving its wings; then one day it was gone, never to reappear. Other birds wheeled and dived near us, uttering short sad cries, but unfortunately we had no bird expert on board – Keith would have known – so they were not identified. I was surprised to find that the *London Book of Verse* did not include the 'Rime of the Ancient Mariner'. I would have liked to learn more about the albatross, who is described somewhere as 'a pious bird of good omen'. We never killed any of the birds we saw, but not because we were ecology-conscious (1960 being a little early for that).

None of them would have been any use to us, besides which the only firearm on board was a rifle that Les had brought with him, presumably to quell any possible mutiny. It was used once, but that was later.

As we progressed across the Pacific our connection with the outer world became increasingly remote. All the radio could do was obtain the time signal for navigation. This isolation didn't worry us because we had created our own little world, enlivened by badinage, private jokes, 'activities' – mainly fishing, all in a framework of necessary routine.

It was on one of these peaceful Pacific nights that my part in the voyage of *Aberdeen Anzac* nearly ended. I was on the wheel, with John as the duty engineer. We were motor-sailing at about four knots, with the engine chuntering along at very low revs, the wind light on the port quarter. John had just gone down into the engine room to check the instruments. As well as steering, I was scrubbing some of the pale purple potatoes we had bought in the Galapagos, and peeling some of them. AA was unusually steady in her movements, so I left the wheel for a moment to throw the potato peelings and scrubbings over the side. Just as I threw the contents of the bucket AA lurched: the bucket went, nearly followed by me had I not managed to grab the mizzen shroud just in time. If I'd gone overboard John wouldn't have heard my shouts in the noise of the engine room, and he might not have come up on deck again for several minutes. Looking back on that episode, it strikes me how very lucky we were. Nobody ever wore a life jacket, not even during the Biscay hurricane, nor did we ever use safety lines. There were some life jackets on board but I do not recall them ever being used. Even allowing for the fact that people were not nearly so safety-conscious in 1960 as they are now, it was all remarkably foolhardy. The whole voyage was an example of how not to embark on such a venture. Carelessness on this scale does not usually go unpunished.

Pam and Muriel made chutney. How? This improbable activity, as I said earlier, is specifically mentioned in my notes made at the time. I can only assume that they decided to use things up, the resultant chutney then being served with the various rice meals that featured so much in our diet – very likely with the tinned pork. Although I don't remember eating it, I do recall the activity in the galley while it was being made, with Bill hanging about hoping for some unconsidered trifle, and being scolded by Muriel.

I discovered much later that we had sailed from Wreck Bay in the nick of time, not because of the impending visit by the Ecuadorian Admiral, but because the very day that we left, May 23rd, was also the day of the great Chilean earthquake which killed about 6,000 people and made 150,000 homeless, in the area of Conception. Of course, we could not learn of it on our nearly useless radio, but one would think that we should have noticed the great tidal wave, travelling at 420 miles per hour, according to the report in *The Times*, which must have passed us as it spread across the Pacific causing damage as far away as Japan, the Soviet far east, the Philippines, Hawaii, New Zealand and the Solomon Islands. It must have taken the shape, as far as we were concerned, of an enormous shallow heave in the surface of the ocean, passing under us quickly and unbrokenly as we continued unawares in our innocent activities. It still seems to me extraordinary that we should have seen and felt nothing, and equally strange that we should have left our anchorage on the very day of the earthquake. If we had lingered one more day we would have known all about it. A great wave such as that, after it had passed, would be likely to suck the sea away after it, dumping us down, hard, on the harbour bottom. Violent contact with the basalt bottom of Wreck Bay would probably have been the end of AA – I don't see how she could have withstood such treatment. We were spared to continue on our charmed way.

In their accounts Robinson, Howard and Hiscock all speak of their awe, in crossing the Pacific, at the sheer distance; what Hiscock describes as 'the tiny daily steps' marked on the chart seemed hardly able to 'reach out far enough to bridge the gap'. Howard writes that 'the vastness of the ocean awes: sometimes I felt human life and effort to be so trivial compared with the eternity of the ocean.' Robinson, after he has pricked off on his chart the first day's 89-mile run from the Galapagos, writes, 'Suddenly, for the first time, I awoke to the full realisation of the enormity of the task ahead of us ... I felt a sudden panic. I felt as a bird might feel, starting out to wing a lonely way to the moon.' I have to confess that I did not share these feelings, nor I think did the rest of the crew of the *Aberdeen Anzac*. Possibly this was because there were more of us, on a larger boat; perhaps too we lacked the imagination to consider more than the daily round. Whatever the reasons we were unawed by the distances we had to travel and I think none felt diminished 'compared with the eternity of the ocean'; but I certainly agreed with Hiscock when I read in *Around the World in Wanderer III*, 'We found the Pacific was more uncomfortable than the homely Atlantic.' The delights of trade-wind sailing were not quite repeated, although the ineffable deep purplish blue was, if anything, even more agreeable to the eye.

Our course being west by south, with a prevailing southeasterly wind, we were running with it broad on the port quarter: this would have been ideal in a sailing yacht but on AA it meant both slowness and a corkscrewing motion. As we neared the Marquesas, the wind lightened to the point when our day's run fell to little over 70 miles under sail alone. Tim announced that we could now run the engine at normal revolutions without risk of using all our diesel before reaching Tahiti.

* * * * *

We had left Wreck Bay on May 23rd; on June 20th we sighted, a black speck on the horizon, Ua Huka, the most easterly of the Marquesas. Muriel expressed surprise that this speck should appear exactly on our stemhead, in precisely the position it should be. Jim was rather vexed: 'Of course it's there – I'm the navigator on this ship.' We stared at Ua Huka as it grew into a proper South Sea island of the volcanic variety: steep cliffs covered in greenery, loud flocks of wheeling seabirds, with a crashing surf. We had no intention of stopping there – we were headed for Taiohae Bay at Nuku Hiva, the official port of entry to the Marquesas. We certainly didn't want to offend any touchy French colonial official by landing at some outlying island before getting proper clearance.

There is something peculiarly chilling about the cry of gulls when echoed back from a cliff face, when one is at sea. Perhaps it is because they seem to be saying 'you're too close – bear away'; which, of course, you are. Many years ago I was cruising in the yacht *Solway Maid* that I have mentioned earlier; we were on passage to Donegal from the Mull of Kintyre and had encountered thick fog in the St George's Channel. The wind had died while we moved slowly forward under power, hearing the fog signal from one of the Rathlin Island lighthouses, hoping to catch a favourable tide to carry us through the Rathlin sound. Sound is distorted in fog; we suddenly heard the loud cry of gulls, seemingly coming from all directions, including directly above us, with a dreadful echoing tone to it which could only indicate cliffs very near at hand. We promptly anchored and waited. Soon the fog lifted and there were the cliffs of Rathlin hardly a stone's throw away. The memory of this incident has stayed with me, dormant but reawakened by that echoing cry of the gulls at Ua Huka.

It would be 'inappropriate' to describe any passage among the islands of the Pacific without any mention of Captain Cook, our greatest navigator. He came to the

Marquesas in the spring of 1774, direct from Easter Island, some 2,300 miles to the southeast. Quite how he knew they were there I couldn't say, but he probably had some idea that if he went in that direction he would find them, even if he depended only on rumour and surmise. Cook was a very lucky seaman. He had been preceded by General Alvaro de Mendana in his flagship galleon *San Geronimo*, in 1595, who was on his way to the Solomon Islands from Peru and thought, when he arrived at the Marquesas, that they *were* the Solomons, but was puzzled that he had reached them so soon. His expedition being under the auspices of the Viceroy of Peru, he named them for his patron, Marquesa del Virrey Garcia Hurtado de Mendoza. He also had even greater authority for his expedition, granted by letters patent signed by Phillip II himself. Naturally, having found the islands, the last people he wanted to know about them were the British, but somehow Cook must have found out that they existed and even worked out roughly where they were.

Anything seemed possible to Cook. He had spent a rather unsatisfactory three weeks at Easter Island. The islanders, like most Pacific islanders, were persistent thieves, besides which 'Nature has been exceedingly spare of favour in this spot', as he noted in his journal. Even water was scarce and Cook, solicitous as always of his crew's health, was anxious to be somewhere where their diet could be improved and supplemented. He hoped for better things at the Marquesas. He sighted the tiny island of Fatu Huku – hardly more than a rock – and named it Hood Island after Alexander Hood, the sixteen-year-old midshipman who saw it first. This lad was advantageously related to Admirals Lord Hood and Lord Bridport (these connections mattered greatly in the eighteenth century, although Cook was not a commander to give them undue weight). Reading his journals can in some respects be rather disappointing in that he makes his great achievements seem quite simple and easy, while, being of a generation before the Romantic movement, he attaches little importance to the description of sublime scenery. One can read long passages in Cook's journal without gaining any impression worth having of the appearance of the dramatic islands he visited.

The Marquesas are roughly apportioned among three groups. Mendana and Cook only visited the southern group, leaving the others to be found by later navigators. Once again, as in most of the places he visited, he found determined thievery, which always infuriated him, but he was greatly impressed by the physical appearance of the islanders. Unfortunately, he was rather disappointed in their eating habits and, as he wasn't able to supplement his sailors' diet as he had hoped, he left for Tahiti after four days, with apparently no regrets.

I have mentioned Cook's luck, which ran out on his third voyage, but it was certainly working well during his rounding of Cape Horn in 1769, when he encountered our old friends the Diego Ramirez isles. Being a prudent commander, with extraordinary prescience in unknown seas, he had continued south from Tierra del Fuego in order to make sure that he had really passed the bottom of the American continent, as far as 60 degrees south, before altering course to the west. Thus he cheated the Diego Ramirez, which he had in view for a couple of days because, his luck still holding, there was a rare calm at the time. Richard Hough, Cook's biographer, describes in a recent book how he himself landed on one of the horrible little group in 1969, from a Chilean gunboat, during a brief spell of good weather. The Chilean navy maintain a weather station there now, where two lonely meteorologists live in a metal hut, being relieved and supplied when the weather permits. I hope they get extra pay for this forlorn posting. Hough tells his readers that 'the vegetation is tussock grass and the birds include three breeds of penguin, ferocious black corvids – 'Johnny Rooks' – and grey headed albatrosses, all amazing to behold'. They were probably equally amazed to behold Mr Hough, as apparently the meteorologists stay in their hut practically all the time.

My ideas of the Marquesas had been formed by Robert Louis Stevenson's *In the South Seas*, Melville's *Typee* and J. B. Priestley's *Faraway*. Of my three yachting voyagers, Hiscock had visited the Marquesas in 1953, Howard in May 1932, while Robinson missed them out altogether. Oddly enough it was J. B. Priestley's *Faraway* that had made the strongest impression. Priestley is little read now, but his description is, to my mind, the best, beside which Stevenson's seems verbose and unfocused. Priestley tells his readers:

> *The Marquesas simply do not belong to this world at all. They were like the ruins of some nobler planet. They transcended any possible order of the picturesque and romantic ... Black crags, pinnacles and tortured promontories had been flung out of the water and piled up in wild confusion; there were jagged peaks lost in cloud, and high smoky valleys; forests were hanging in the air, dripping and glittering; and rising sheer from the green depths were immense dark walls where innumerable white threads of waterfall were swaying and a hundred thousand white birds went circling. Every island seemed to have just been plucked from the very heart of the sea, so that it was still dripping with salt water. They were black mountains and dark green woods for ever seen through a mist of spray. They were Gothic castles of the deep Pacific ... They were terrifying, beautiful, beautiful, and incredible.*

This might sound to the reader today like a stage direction for *Gormenghast*, but I have quoted it at length because Priestley describes very much my own impression of Nuku Hiva. We moved along the south coast of the island at a distance of about 200 yards – or, if I am to be relentlessly nautical, one cable. There were the wavering waterfalls tumbling down into the sea, with the trade wind blowing them sideways in fans of spray, and the wheeling gulls crying as we passed. After a month at sea it was an amazing sight – it would have been an amazing sight at any time. Priestley's book was published in 1930, when the world was not as ruthlessly travelled as it is now and a visit to the Marquesas would have been a difficult enterprise. It may be that today there is an airstrip on Nuku Hiva, possibly even a chain hotel. As we moved slowly along the line of cliffs I could see no sign of human habitation, nor any indication that the island had been discovered at all. Its population was a great deal less than it had been two hundred years earlier; it seemed to have recovered its pristine state.

We identified the Sentinel Rocks marking the entrance to Taiohae Bay, the only place of any consequence, if consequence is measured in number of houses, on the island. After dropping our anchor near the end of the jetty we sat about on deck, dazed by the sun and buffeting wind, and had a cup of tea to celebrate our arrival. We were in an amphitheatre of green mountains; it was a faery land, just as Priestley had described. I think we all felt like the Lotos-Eaters in Tennyson's poem:

> *All round the coast the languid air did swoon,*
> *Breathing like one that hath a weary dream,*
> *Full-faced above the valley stood the moon;*
> *And like a downward smoke, the slender stream*
> *Along the cliff to fall and pause and fall did seem.*

Tennyson seems to have had some sympathy with the crew of AA, which is odd because I hadn't thought of him as a particularly nautical person. When reading 'The Lotos-Eaters' and coming upon the lines

> *We have had enough of action, and of motion we,*
> *Rolled to starboard, rolled to larboard,*

When the surge was seething free,
Where the wallowing monster spouted
His foam-fountains in the sea

— I thought, well, perhaps not Tennyson at his best, but relevant to the feelings of us all when we dropped anchor off Nuku Hiva.

* * * * *

However, curiosity and practical necessity soon overcame the dreamy atmosphere. In order to call on the French Resident we rowed ashore with Les, landing at the official jetty. The foreshore was park-like, with a bright greensward on the seaward side of a dirt road running along in front of a few houses, but there were no people to be seen. We found a tennis court and a small post office; eventually a Frenchman appeared who was clearly in some official capacity. He disappeared with Les while Bill and I walked along the road in search of a place where we could buy some provisions. After about 100 yards we passed a couple of fellows, each pushing a wheelbarrow; they seemed to be repairing a culvert at the roadside. It transpired later that they were convicts who, so far as I was able to ascertain, were the only labour force on Nuku Hiva. Nothing much seemed to have changed since R. L. Stevenson's visit aboard the schooner *Casco* about 70 years before, except that there seemed to be rather fewer people around. He too had met convicts with wheelbarrows, working in the Residency gardens.

The whole place was dripping with moisture and steamy hot, with a backdrop of mist-wreathed mountains. We were in search of a 'trader' who we had been told would sell us provisions. This was Bob McKettrick. I knew something about him because I had read of him in Hiscock's book, in which there is a photograph of him 'spinning a yarn'. I was apprehensive that he might prove a dreadful bore with his 'yarns', particularly as Hiscock had given what I took to be a warning: 'with Bob you never can tell whether he is pulling your leg or not; he is a great spinner of yarns and as he chatters on with an accent oddly reminiscent of France and Liverpool there is always a twinkle in his eye.' I was fully expecting to meet a cross between the Ancient Mariner and the worst sort of pub bore, eager to dump endless anecdotes on us. We found him, sitting on his veranda as if he had been waiting there since Hiscock had departed, seven years before. His Polynesian wife lurked in the background. I muttered to Bill that we'd come to buy provisions, not to hear reminiscences.

In the event I was quite wrong (I often am): the yarn that he spun for us was fascinating, being about his time in Tahiti at the beginning of the 1914–18 war. Bob had total recall. The French governor had come down into Papeete, the capital, in his official carriage, drawn by a pair of matched horses, to announce the outbreak of hostilities to the assembled and no doubt bemused Tahitians. During his proclamation he became quite animated, standing up in the carriage to gesticulate (all this in full ceremonial uniform complete with cocked hat). Bob had seen all this and told the story with relish. The good people of Tahiti were puzzled – what could the Archduke Ferdinand or the Alsace–Lorraine question have meant to them? – but enthusiastic. I wondered if the Governor had formed a militia to counter the threat of a landing from the German Pacific Squadron; Bob thought not. I imagined a sort of Tahitian Dad's Army – or rather, to be strictly truthful, I have imagined it since because Dad's Army had not been mustered in 1960 – armed with spears, led by the chiefs (Polynesia is, or was, full of chiefs). This episode was not quite the comic-opera event that one might suppose; in September 1914, Admiral von Spee, in command of the Imperial Pacific Fleet, bombarded Tahiti, for no very good reason, on his way to Chile. Possibly he was registering the effectiveness of his guns but he might have done better to preserve his ammunition for the battles of Coronel and the Falklands.

Bob sat on his verandah in his rocking chair, with his smiling little wife in the background (I wonder how often she'd heard his stories), a delightful domestic scene. I wish I'd photographed it but I had no camera, a lack that I've always regretted. He didn't have much to sell; he was an old man by 1960, more concerned with spinning yarns than with serious commercial activity, but we bought a large bag of green coffee beans for which I blessed him later, and some cans of beer. As we walked back to the jetty, carrying our beer and beans, the sight of a horse tethered in the grassy yard of a hut gave me the idea of an island expedition on horseback. The owner agreed to hire the animal to me and to find others if more of us wanted to join me (this conversation was conducted in schoolboy French, a much easier language than real French). Bill said he didn't want to have anything to do with horses. Back on board, I found that Dick was keen to come; we arranged to go next day with a local guide and a picnic, up into the mountains.

We set off mounted on wooden saddles which, although practical, are remarkably hard on the bottom. Our guide promised us that when we reached a certain height we would enjoy what an earlier generation would have called extensive views. We climbed steadily by a muddy track, passing evidence of dwellings which had nearly disappeared in the undergrowth – stone platforms on which the huts were once built. The path wound among huge boulders, nearly losing itself in places. The heat was oppressive; the horses were listless and did not share our enthusiasm for the outing. We could see nothing but the dense greenery around us – all we knew was that we were climbing and would eventually emerge above the tree line. This was quite possibly the same path that Herman

Melville took after he deserted from the whaler *Dolly* at Taiohae in the summer of 1842. (*Dolly* is the name he gives the ship in *Typee*; it seems the real name was *Acushnet*.) The French Admiral du Petit Thouars had just taken possession of the islands and his squadron was anchored in the bay at the time of Melville's desertion. Finally we reached a break in the trees and could look down at a scene which had changed little since Melville described it, rather extravagantly:

> *The lonely bay of Nukuheva, dotted here and there with the black hulls of the vessels composing the French squadron, lay reposing at the base of a circular range of elevations, whose verdant sides, perforated with deep glens, or diversified with smiling valleys, formed altogether the loveliest scene I ever beheld, and were I to live a hundred years, I shall never forget the feeling of admiration which I then experienced.*

Well, I shall not compete with that, but it was certainly a fine sight. In contrast, Melville displays a touch of pawky New England humour in his mention of a characteristic of the Marquesans which I recognised: 'It is a peculiarity among these people, that when engaged in any employment they always make a prodigious fuss about it. So seldom do they exert themselves, that when they do work they seem determined that so meritorious an action shall not escape the observation of those around.' I know that the Marquesans we met were not the true Marquesans of Melville's day. They all disappeared, destroyed over the years by disease, and were replaced by the present population, such as it is – immigrants from Tahiti and elsewhere – but some of the characteristics he noticed have transferred to the present inhabitants; or perhaps they are merely shared by all Polynesians. Certainly, as we found later in Papeete, if one wanted, say, a shirt made, it was no use expecting a Tahitian to do it: the Chinese were the people who actually *did* things. The native Tahitians seemed not to resent this immigrant commercial enterprise – unlike the Fijians' apparent resentment of the Indian enterprise in their islands.

It was slow going up the side of Nuku Hiva on our sulky horses; I thought they would be more enthusiastic on the way back. After about two hours we emerged onto a delightful open area of grass blowing in the trade wind. A herd of wild horses ran across the waving grass about three hundred yards further up the sloping valley side. They may not have been wild, they may have belonged to someone – things usually do – but they were acting wild, with their manes blowing in the wind in an abandoned manner, as in those films, once popular, of the white horses of the Camargue. On all sides except that of the cliffs overlooking the sea were the flanks of mountains rising to peaks of about 4,000 feet. We rode at the edge of the cliffs, looking down onto the backs of gulls wheeling below. In all this time, apart from the ruins of old buildings that we had seen at the outset, there had been no sign of humanity. It was midwinter, the rainy season; the waterfalls were in fullest spate, but we could not hear them because of the buffeting of the wind. In a weird way, the scene resembled the English Lake District, and I said as much to Dick. 'Nearly as wet, too,' he answered. We walked our horses along the edge of a cliff overlooking the sea for about half a mile, then stopped, thinking of our picnic. It was blessedly cool up there, the trade wind having combined with the altitude to disperse the heavy atmosphere of the coast. Never had I been anywhere which felt as remote as these Marquesan uplands. I believe Dick shared my sudden inclination to yell and charge across the grasslands, like cowboys, but our horses did not share these feelings so we dismounted for our picnic instead.

Our guide told us, as we were eating, that it would start raining very soon, and we could see the rain clouds gathering on the mountains to the east, so we hurriedly finished and climbed back onto our hard wooden saddles. I could not decide whether Nuku Hiva was enchanted or cursed – maybe it was both. There was certainly something of the sinister lying in the beauty of the place, but this may have been due to a knowledge of the cannibalism that had been practised in the islands until comparatively recently. Stevenson has a good deal to say about it in his *In the South Seas*. He recounts that even as late as the time of his visit in 1888, the natives were still occasionally eating each other in spite of French rule and the influence of the Roman Catholic priests. There was a particularly macabre incident in which

> *the people of a valley seized and slew a wretch who had offended them. His offence, it is to be supposed, was dire; they could not bear to leave their vengeance incomplete, and, under the eyes of the French, did not dare to hold a public festival. The body was accordingly divided; and every man retired to his own house to consummate the rite in secret, carrying his proportion of the dreadful meat in a Swedish match-box.*

Stevenson is alive to the gruesome absurdity of the ceremony, the removal of the 'dreadful meat' in Swedish matchboxes, just as pieces of wedding cake are taken away wrapped in Kleenex: as he puts it, 'The barbarous substance of the drama and the European properties employed offer a seizing contrast to the imagination.' The cannibal proclivities of the various Polynesian and Melanesian ethnic groups obviously interested him greatly:

> *Cannibalism is traced from end to end of the Pacific, from the Marquesas to New Guinea, from New Zealand to Hawaii, here in the lively haunt of its exercise, there by scanty but significant survivals ... All Melanesia appears tainted. In Micronesia, in the Marshalls ... I could find no trace at all; and even in the Gilbert zone I long looked and asked in vain ... The higher Polynesian races, such as the Tahitians, Hawaiians, and Samoans, had one and all outgrown, and some of them had in part forgot, the practice, before Cook or Bougainville had shown a topsail in their waters. It lingered only in some low islands where life was difficult to maintain, and among inveterate savages like the New Zealanders or the Marquesans.*

Such a history, attaching to Nuku Hiva, is bound to have some effect on the ambience of a place, however entrancing to look at.

Soon after we left our grassy plateau to return to Taiohae by the muddy path the heavens opened and soon turned it into a torrent. Our horses, so far from being enthusiastic about going home, became even more intractable. It seemed simpler to dismount and pull them along behind us; more comfortable too, as the wet wooden saddles chafed the backside. So we retraced our way, slipping and sliding in the muddy river until we reached Taiohae. As we advanced into the village, back in the saddle, there was Tim standing in the middle of the road. It had stopped raining; he had his camera in his hand. 'Give us a cavalry charge and I'll take your picture,' he shouted, so we kicked our mounts into a reluctant trot. Tim was pleased. 'You were tall in the saddle,' he said, and disappeared.

The owner of the horses was also a wood carver, specialising in bowls that he covered in complicated designs, and I was so taken with his work that I bought one. I still have it; it contains, or has contained over the last forty years, paper clips, bicycle tyre valves, puncture repair outfits, curtain rings, drawing pins and, more recently, assorted coins. It is my sole evidence of Marquesan skills.

Back on board AA, after putting on some dry clothes, I decided to make some coffee from the green beans I had bought from Bob McKettrick. First I roasted the beans in a large pan over the Calor gas cooker, then I ground them coarsely, and made the coffee immediately afterwards. It was delicious, very strong, and gave everyone the shakes.

Having got clearance from the Resident, we were free to go anywhere in the island group. We decided to move further along the coast to Comptroller Bay. Pam thought this would be a good opportunity to get on a horse, follow along to our new anchorage, keeping near sea level, and join us at Comptroller Bay. This would have worked well except that our departure was delayed for reasons now forgotten, so that when she got to the bay there was no sign of us. The local chief put her up without question and by the time we arrived she was having a good time and was in no hurry to rejoin AA; so Les went ashore and they both spent a further three days with the chief. The part of the coast where we lay had been, apparently, the seaward end of the Taipee valley made known by Melville in *Typee*. There was of course no evidence of that at the time of our visit, but there was evidence of the tidal wave that had swept the Pacific after the Chilean earthquake the previous month. It wasn't as impressive as I had hoped. The frequent heavy rainstorms had washed away most of the mud; nature recovers quickly in such lush areas. Nor was there much sign of habitation, apart from the pathetic little platforms that had once supported huts. Those three days we spent anchored at Comptroller Bay, off the Taipee valley, are strangely lost to me. The sun shone, the surf crashed on the beach, the trees swayed and bent to the trade wind, the seabirds cried as they wheeled about the cliffs; it was all as if in a dream, reminding me, again, of Tennyson's Lotos-Eaters. One can easily understand those men who are washed up in Polynesia and become beachcombers. It's not a part of the world that will sharpen your wits.

Before leaving Nuku Hiva I should mention one particular unpleasantness that we were, for unknown reasons, spared: the nono fly. Both Hiscock and Howard make special mention of the pest. Hiscock's wife Susan suffered greatly, counting no less than 97 bites on one leg alone, while Howard writes: 'And the nono fly? This little fellow is very tiny – about the size of a small ant – and his bite is out of all proportion to his size. He is a native of Nuku Hiva only and does not appear to pester the other islands. We were bitten and found the result worse than the bite of a mosquito.' This fly did not trouble us, possibly because the French government had done something about it between the times of Hiscock's visit in 1953 and ours in 1960. It may be that something in our diet made us unattractive to the nono – and I can recall no annoyance from mosquitoes either.

* * * * *

On June 26th we sailed for Ua Pou, forty miles to the south. The trade wind was blowing briskly, from east by north, so that we were able to set our rig. As I hauled the booms of the twin headsails round to catch it, the starboard boom, pinned down by its kicking strap, promptly broke – a serious matter as we had no replacement. Nigel was obliged to bring out his leather tool bag and 'fish' it. By this I mean that he joined the two parts together with a strengthening piece across the join with clever fashioning of the two broken halves. It lasted for the rest of the voyage, but I eased the kicking strap to reduce the strain on it.

Ua Pou is the most extraordinary island. RLS, seeing it from the deck of *Casco*, wrote:

> *The first rays of the sun displayed the needles of Ua-Pu. These pricked about the line of the horizon; like the pinnacles of some ornate and monstrous church, they stood there, in the sparkling brightness of the morning, the fit signboard of a world of wonders.*

I won't compete with RLS – to me they seemed like a child's drawing of 'the island of the goblin king'. I don't think anyone could call Ua Pou beautiful. It is bizarre. The Marquesas are volcanic; these strange peaks must have been thrown up in eruption long ago and, being of harder rock than the surrounding land, had gradually been exposed, like great teeth, over the millennia. Jim and Dave thought they would climb them, or one at least. There being no obvious harbour at Ua Pou we dropped anchor off a shelving sandy beach, where we could see several other craft. No sooner was our anchor down than we had visitors. A group of small boys suddenly leapt over AA's bulwarks, darting about the deck, diving down into the cabins and, before we could stop them, snatching up anything that was lying about. Fortunately, it being AA, there wasn't much to steal, but they got half a packet of cigarettes – mine – from the table in the fo'c'sle and had some luck in the aft cabin, managing to collect some of Nigel's cigarette tobacco and a can of beer from Bill's bunk. I saw a furious red-faced Muriel chasing one boy out of the galley, straight over the side into the water where he swam to a canoe. It was like a scene from *Mutiny on the Bounty*, except that they were all boys. The girls seemed not to be interested in stealing or else they weren't allowed to join in.

Ua Pou was very different from Nuku Hiva: more populated – huts were dotted all over the place – and altogether more cheerful and lively. We landed in our dinghy through the surf onto a fine, gently sloping sandy beach. Jim and Dave set off to climb one of the strange tooth-like mountains. It was hard to see how they could even start – the sides were sheer, smooth, and seemed free of any ledges. I told Jim that in the event of their not returning he should not hope for a search party from AA. He said that the thought had never crossed his mind.

The day after our arrival we learnt that there was going to be a barbecue, organised by some Americans from a couple of the yachts anchored offshore. We were told there would be roast sucking pig and other delicacies, beer, rum, and whisky. We seemed to have arrived at the right time. For some reason, probably because as the only 'yachtsman' on board, rowing was considered to be my province, I was expected to row everybody ashore, in a ferry service. Now anyone who has ever landed or launched a dinghy through surf will know that it is important to keep the hull at right angles to the line of the breaking waves. The surf at Ua Pou was not formidable – nothing like the sort of terrifying breakers that you see in films of surfers doing their stuff on the Australian coast. It was more like Cardigan Bay on a day of stiff breeze. The landings went well, but after the party, launching was strangely difficult. Twice the dinghy rolled over, pitching the foolishly giggling passengers into the sea. It took a long time to fetch the whole crew back to AA, in the magical darkness, with phosphorescence at every dip of the oars. Of the roast pig banquet I remember that we sat on the ground in a big circle; the Americans, various unknown invitees, the crew of the *Aberdeen Anzac* – about forty people in all. Les wore his captain's hat and was served first.

It has always puzzled me that none of my three yachtsman–navigators visited Ua Pou. It is odd that in the case of Hiscock and Howard the extraordinary sight of it did not arouse their curiosity enough to pull them in. Howard writes: 'Of all the islands it is the most beautiful. Never have I seen such amazing pinnacles, towers, castles, obelisks and queer faces as in that marvel of the Marquesas.' Robinson avoided the whole Marquesan group, so his circumstances were different. I suspect that the lure of Tahiti had taken over by the time he had come so far, or he may have needed stores and fuel urgently. Robert Louis Stevenson oddly records no landing – he of all people! He describes his closest approach:

> *We skirted the windward shore of that indescribable island of Ua Pou; viewing with dizzy eyes [he was feeling sea sick] the coves, the capes, the breakers, the climbing forests, and the inaccessible stone needles that surmount the mountains. The place persists, in a dark corner of our memories, like a piece of the scenery of nightmares.*

For someone who has just described the place as 'indescribable', he does well in his description. When the *Casco* reached her destination – Hiva Oa – their landing was like what it would have been at Ua Pou if they had stopped there: 'The surf ran high ... the boat broached to and capsized; and all hands were submerged.'

The day after the feast was the day of the *Aberdeen Anzac* goat hunt. We had seen several goats on the cliffs as we approached the island and, on the assumption that they were wild, it seemed a good idea to shoot one in order to vary our diet. Les the Hunter produced the rifle that was our sole weapon on board, and embarked in the dinghy in search of a goat to shoot. I did not take part in this expedition but I heard all about it afterwards. The hunting party rowed along under the cliffs, just outside the line of surf, until a large goat was seen perched on a ledge near the top of the cliff face. Les steadied himself in the middle of the dinghy and shot it. It fell into the sea where it was recovered, dead. The hunters returned in triumph to AA and the unfortunate goat was prepared for eating. That same afternoon we heard that every goat belonged to someone, and that if the gendarme heard of our exploit we might well be in trouble. Life on Ua Pou was not, apparently, quite so free and arcadian as we had imagined. Dave said that Les would probably be arrested and sent to work with the other convicts, repairing the road on Nuku Hiva. He had escaped at Chatham Island, but would get his come-uppance in the Marquesas, ending his days as a convict. Hard labour for Les, that was the common opinion. 'He won't like that,' said John, somewhat superfluously. 'What about his aiders and abettors?' asked Nigel, 'I didn't go in the boat, but you did, didn't you, John?' 'Nothing to do with me – I don't like goat,' said Dick. The general consensus was that we should leave Ua Pou as soon as possible. Jim and Dave had made their predictably abortive attempt to climb one of the stone needles, so there was nothing to detain us.

* * * * *

We weighed anchor shortly after dawn and made our way under power round the leeward side of the island before shaping a course for Tahiti, a thousand miles to the southwest. The trades were blowing freshly on our port quarter so as soon as we were clear I set our rig. Once again the headsails were angled to the best effect, Big Jib pulled well as always, the mizzen sheet was hardened in together with its topsail, and the very frail spare mizzen was hoisted in front of the wheelhouse. This somewhat obscured the helmsman's view forward, but as we sailed on a compass course, I don't recall any complaints about that. We quickly fell into our ocean routine, but without any of the small luxuries, such as biscuits and jam, which we had enjoyed in our earlier days; all that sort of thing had been consumed and it was spartan rations from now on. Jim had laid a course to take us through the Tuamotus, passing close to Rangiroa, leaving that island to starboard. I was nervous about this. The Tuamotus are coral islands, low-lying to the point of being invisible at more than about six miles; I had a persistent fear of being surprised at night by roaring surf and disaster. I needn't have worried. Jim had estimated correctly that we would pass by Rangiroa in daylight; sure enough, we saw its palm trees lined up on our horizon all day as we moved along at about four knots.

I'm not sure why coral islands concerned me so much. I think I was beginning to feel that our luck had held too long – we had survived comparatively unscathed for eight months. I thought something dire was due to happen, and indeed it did, but not at all the sort of thing that I expected. Dave had cut his leg making his hopeless attempt to climb one of the Ua Pou peaks with Jim. This cut had started to fester. Tim had managed to cut himself somewhere on Nuku Hiva, and this had not healed. Muriel was worried; our medical box was pitifully inadequate. As we were at least five days away from Tahiti the possibility of blood poisoning was grim. It would have been unwise to stop at one of the Tuamotu islands because we had no idea what medical help we could expect at any of them. As usual, we had assumed that nothing would ever be the matter with us, when of course the risk of trouble is greater in the tropics. Poor Dave sat perched on the gunwale like a sick starling, saying very little, stoical as always. Tim suffered too, but as his injury was less spectacular than Dave's he secured less sympathy. Looking back, I wonder how it was that we were so foolishly sanguine, and I can only assume that we had to be. If we had admitted to ourselves that we should do this, that and the other about our health we would never have started. We couldn't afford to do more, so we shut our minds to the possibility of danger. Our diet was no help: pork in tins was not very nourishing, we had run out of porridge, the corn flakes had become limp and musty, we were all sick of the tinned milk, and the rice was infested with some species of mite. We did, at least, have unlimited tea.

In ordinary circumstances the Tuamotus would have 'beckoned' as we motor-sailed through them, Rangiroa to starboard with its long line of palm trees. But any delay was out of the question. Tim calculated that we had ample fuel to reach Papeete, so Dick raised the engine revolutions to give us near maximum speed, even at the risk of blowing the gasket again.

Stevenson's description of the Tuamotus is not encouraging, either from a navigational or from a social point of view. The captain of the *Casco* had been persuaded against his better judgement to sail among the islands (RLS calls them the Puamotus, but it is the same place – Polynesian spelling is erratic) and had signed on a pilot at Taiohae. This man, the only one in the ship's company who had any experience of these waters, loses his way among the atolls so that *Casco* is forced to change course continually in order to dodge the many coral reefs. RLS writes:

> *In no quarter are the atolls so thickly congregated, in none are they so varied in size from the greatest to the least, and in none is navigation so beset with perils, as in that archipelago that we were now to thread. The huge system of the trades is, for some reason, quite confounded by this multiplicity of reefs; the wind intermits, squalls are frequent from the west and south-west, hurricanes are known ... The currents are, besides, inextricably intermixed; dead reckoning becomes farce; the charts are not to be trusted; as such is the number and similarity of these islands that, even when you have picked one up, you may be none the wiser ... I believe, indeed, it is almost*

understood that yachts are to avoid this baffling archipelago.

That was written seventy years before our arrival. I understand from Hiscock's book that the French navy resurveyed the Tuamotus not long before our visit, and our charts were probably based on that survey. Nevertheless, it is an unnerving part of the watery world, conducive to hallucination and eyestrain.

Jim didn't seem in the least bothered; his confidence infected us. By this time, he enjoyed the reputation and status of the master navigator, the infallible fixer of position, even though in fact our navigational methods and equipment were little better than those on board the *Casco*. She, of course, had no radio, but her chronometer was no doubt as reliable as ours, so we had not much advantage except that of being able to get a time signal. Up-to-date, accurate charts are essential to the navigator, but even they could not tell us, or anyone, how strong the currents are going to be, or in what direction they will flow. Not for nothing are the Tuamotus sometimes called the Dangerous Isles. Most visitors tend to get lost, even if only for a short time. Robinson manages to get seriously adrift in his approach, nearly losing *Svaap* in the process. The atolls seem to shift about in the sea, just as the spellings change from book to book. Even the very experienced and undaunted Hiscock – a role model for the cruising yachtsman – confesses to alarm at the confusions of the Tuamotus, and in the event he is unable to land at any of them. The current flowing out of the lagoons is too fast for his low-powered engine, while the passes are too narrow to beat in under sail. Regretfully he sails on for Tahiti. Howard, with his usual insouciance, stops at Takaroa for a month. Here he helped a pearl fisher garner his pearls, or, to be more accurate, he watched the old women who opened the oysters to make sure that they didn't steal any pearls.

Unsurprisingly it is RLS who tells us of the sinister – indeed evil – aspect of the South Sea islands. He has already told us about the cannibalism of the Marquesas, but it is in the Tuamotus that we hear of mean and vengeful practices of which the Marquesans would probably not have been guilty. He found that there was something innately wrong with coral islands. At the time of his visit, Fakarava was the seat of government of the Tuamotus, chosen because the lagoon has two entrances or passes from the outer ocean. Much delights RLS during his stay at Fakarava, but he rather spoils the effect by telling us that the fish are liable to be poisonous and finishes his description of the place with an alarming paragraph: 'It adds a last touch of horror to the thought of this precarious annular gangway in the sea, that even what there is of it is not of honest rock, but organic, part alive part putrescent; even the clean sea and the bright fish about it poisoned, the most stubborn boulder burrowed in by worms, the lightest dust venomous as an apothecary's drugs.' As for the character of the islanders, this left much to be desired. Elephantiasis had taken hold on the island of Makatea, and those suffering from it were confined to a reserved part, from which they would creep early in the morning 'into the sleeping village, and stealthily make water at the doors of the houses of young men. Thus they propagate disease ... Whether horrid fact or more abominable legend, it equally depicts that something bitter and energetic which distinguished Paumotuan man.'

Once clear of the islands, we were able to alter course slightly, making direct for Tahiti. Most travellers approach the place with expectations of South Sea delights, but I think I speak for all the crew of AA when I say that our main concern was to get to an efficient doctor and hospital – it could have been Liverpool for all we cared. I have a strangely muffled memory of this passage. I spent nearly all my time on deck or in the wheelhouse – there was no temptation to go below except to sleep. It was far too hot and stuffy in either the fo'c'sle or the aft cabin – North Sea trawler accommodation is not designed for tropic use. I fiddled with the set of the sails, although it could have made little or no difference to our speed. At dusk on July 1st the mountain peaks of Tahiti appeared as specks on the horizon. We stood off until dawn, then went in to moor stern-to at Papeete town quay.

* * * * *

Noise was our immediate impression of Papeete. After weeks of a complete absence of traffic, the stream of cars, vans, scooters and mopeds had a dazing effect. Dave and Tim went straight up to the local hospital, where, it being a weekend, there was no doctor. But they were treated by an enormous Tahitian nurse who injected them, presumably with some antibiotic, and told them to come back on Monday to see Doctor. Pam went ashore with our rice, and gave it as a present to a Chinese woman who tipped it into a large shallow dish, then picked out the weevils by hand, one by one. I suppose we could have done that, but no one had the stomach for it; so far as we were concerned, the rice was condemned. That evening, Bill and I went ashore to look for a particular restaurant. More than three years before, a young Frenchman had joined *Gratitude*, briefly, with the intention of coming with us to Tahiti in order to start what he had told us would be the best restaurant in French Polynesia. He had taken one look at *Gratitude*, spent one night on board, and then decided to go to Papeete by a Messageries Maritimes liner instead. I told Bill that if we could find the restaurant, whose existence I really doubted, we could probably get a free meal. The Frenchman's plans had seemed just the sort of romantic dream most doomed to non-fruition, but to my amazement there he was in his restaurant, which did indeed have the reputation of being the best in Tahiti, therefore in French Polynesia. I had a very friendly reunion with the proprietor and we had a fine meal, but it wasn't free. It was the best meal we had in Papeete; not repeated, so we didn't grudge the expense.

We found that all the commerce of Papeete was in the hands of Chinese. I suppose one could have discovered Tahitian enterprise, but it was certainly not noticeable. If, for example, anyone wanted to have a shirt made, it could be done at a couple of hours' notice in a Chinese shop. Soon after we had arrived in the port, it became apparent that some important event was planned. The yachts in the harbour were dressed overall and at first I was puzzled, until it suddenly dawned on me that we were approaching Bastille Day, July 14th. This national celebration is a great fete day in Polynesia, with displays of dancing, canoe races and general excitement involving crowds of visitors from other islands. We decided that it would be a pity to miss the fun, even though there was no other reason for us to stay until the 14th. We didn't leave until the 20th and that, as it turned out, was a mistake. We lay in our berth for more than two weeks as the festivities intensified. There was a smart light-grey French cruiser lying further along the waterfront. As I stood admiring her, the officer of the watch on the quarterdeck in his formal whites caught my eye and gave me an exaggerated wink as if to say, 'We have to put on a good show for the natives.' Big teams of dancers practised their dances over and over again in a public park beside the road, to the accompaniment of incessant drumming. Tim and Dave took no pleasure in all this fun. They went back to see Doctor at the hospital and Dave told me that he had suffered greatly at the hands of the woman on duty. She had scooped out rotting flesh from his putrescent wound – that was about as much as I wanted to hear. Tim was not such a serious case, but both of them had to make more visits to the hospital before they were pronounced fit.

Added to all the Bastille Day preparations was the excitement of a film company shooting *Mutiny on the Bounty*, featuring Trevor Howard and Marlon Brando. Their activities did not impinge on us in any way, save that Brando could sometimes be seen stumbling along the waterfront after a drinking session, and shrieks were heard from members of the company who had been invited aboard a yacht a few berths along from us. And the prices in the smarter waterside bars were raised.

Tahiti is shaped like a figure of eight, with a large round part joined by a narrow isthmus to a smaller part of similar shape. The large part is about 20 miles across, rising to over 7,000 feet, being the cone of an old volcano; while the smaller part, another old volcano, is about 8 miles across and over 4,000 feet. A coral reef surrounds the whole island. In 1960 there wasn't a road going round the whole island, but there was one which took you down to the southern tip (Papeete being in the north). Here there was a hotel comprising a collection of huts. I hired a moped, one of those devices driven by a small petrol engine mounted above the front wheel. This arrangement depends on a reasonably new front tyre, which has to take the drive. My vehicle had a very old, worn front tyre, but I was able to rent it cheaply in consequence. This sort of gamble rarely works out satisfactorily, nor did it on this occasion. On my first day I drove down to the hotel and all went well. All the local people were milling about, waiting for the cinema to start. It was a western starring John Wayne: he is, or was, very popular in Tahiti and the cinema was packed – every seat taken. Early the next morning, I walked a few yards down to the edge of the lagoon, where tiny waves were breaking on a sandy shore. The reef surrounding the island at a distance of one to two miles from the coast rules out the possibility of any grand oceanic breakers.

On the way back to Papeete I stopped to buy something to eat at a village shop. Parked outside was a large, luxurious American touring car – an unusual sight, so unusual that I hung about to see who would get into it. Eventually an American in a floral shirt, accompanied by a small girl of about ten, who looked as if she might be his daughter, climbed into the car and started unwrapping some chocolate, then dividing it with evident delight. The man seemed familiar, and after a minute it dawned on me who he was: my hero, William Albert Robinson. The very attractive small girl with her large dark eyes and an olive complexion was, I guessed, half Polynesian. I recognised Robinson from the photograph of him in *Deep Water and Shoal* taken thirty years before, sitting in the cabin of *Svaap*. He looked up, and may well have wondered why this strange fellow was gazing at him. Perhaps he thought I was admiring his enchanting-looking child, but at any rate he smiled in a friendly manner before addressing again the matter of the chocolate and its division. Later, I was to see his fine schooner *Varua* in the harbour and later still I read his book *To the Great Southern Ocean*, but it wasn't a patch on *Deep Water*. On the last stretch back into Papeete there was a loud flabby bang as my front tyre exploded – altogether expected. Fortunately I only had to push the machine about half a mile to the garage I had rented it from, where a long argument in French about compensation ensued. In the normal way I wouldn't have bothered, but every franc counted. In the end I got a few, very few, francs back from the *garagiste*.

Robinson, Hiscock and Howard all made lengthy stops at Tahiti – it is the Piccadilly Circus of the South Sea islands. Robinson stayed for eight months on his round-the-world voyage, Hiscock for three weeks, while Howard sold his boat *Pacific Moon* to a young Argentinian for what he estimated to be half her value. I wonder. My experience as a yacht broker had taught me that yacht owners often feel they have sold their craft for half what they are worth when in fact a yacht will sell for what someone will pay, and that is what it is worth. I have always felt that I saw Tahiti at the very end of its old style; at a point when those aspects which had made it peculiarly Tahiti were already crumbling, but still recognisable and about to be destroyed. I walked out to a headland one morning to look down on the building of the new international airport. Graders and dump trucks were moving about and one could already see the outlines of the runway-to-be. As soon as large-bodied aircraft full of tourists could arrive every day, that, I felt, would be the end of Tahiti; I have never been back to find out. One got a foretaste of what it would be like when the airport opened, when the cruise ship came in. A very large American liner arrived for an overnight stop while we were in the harbour; the whole place seethed for about twenty-four hours; that, I guessed, might be its permanent state soon when it could boast an airport. The waterfront was in any case very lively because of July 14th. All the yachts were dressed overall and even AA had hoisted her international code flags. She looked rather ridiculous, like an elephant in a tutu.

Nigel and John had decided to leave AA and take passage direct to Sydney. They felt that they had been away from their wives for long enough, and it was about time they started earning again. Nigel had been aboard since October – nearly nine months; it was high time that he organised his home in Queensland. With no idea that it would take so long to reach New Zealand, he had married shortly before sailing from Southwick, while John, who had joined AA in December, was also needed at home in Brisbane. So they went together to the Messageries Maritimes office in Papeete to buy tickets on the *Tahitien*, due into port shortly before July 14th.

I was curious to hear all about this, to me, enviable chance to sail on a passenger liner, so I questioned them closely about their experience at the booking office. Nigel explained in his inimitable Nigel manner. The booking clerk had gradually moved down through the classes available, reciting the ticket prices, until they finally reached rock bottom: 'dormitory' class at £53. I warned them that this was probably like boarding school, with lights out and beatings if they were found out of their beds at incorrect hours. Nigel said that whatever it was, it was sure to be an improvement on *Aberdeen Anzac*, at least they'd get fed, even if it was only with the leavings from the higher-class tables. John had the decency to say that they would miss my porridge and Nigel added that he would be able to bear that with equanimity. When the *Tahitien* docked and I went on board to see what was in store for them, I said that I would rather stay on AA. There seemed to be little chance that they would be able to see the sea or sky, or get any fresh air. Their dormitory was close to a loading chute for cement, which I predicted would cover them with fine dust. I pointed out that on AA, even though the food had become almost insupportable, we could always take a walk round the deck. John returned, as a clincher, that *Tahitien* had the advantage of being reasonably certain to arrive at Sydney on due date. In any case by this time they had bought their tickets and committed themselves.

Their impending departure had a depressing effect on the rest of us; I knew that I was going to miss them greatly – both Nigel's dry sense of humour and John's good-natured, abrupt manner. They were a sort of 'turn', the pair of them: Nigel the iconoclast, the disparager, John the sensible make-the-best-of-it Nigel-minder. They habitually smoked each other's cigarettes, with endless wrangling about whose they actually were, how many each owed the other; in their continuing duo they were a diversion to us all, particularly to Tim, who studied them as if they were a strange antipodean phenomenon, which indeed they were.

The day the *Tahitien* sailed was a gloomy one. Tim and I went to watch her leave. She slowly edged away from the quayside, with a great, sad, sonorous blast on her siren. We could see no sign of Nigel or John. Tim said that they were probably battened down below; Messageries Maritimes were not going to waste valuable deck space that might be required for higher-class passengers. There is always a poignancy about the departure of an ocean-going passenger boat which is quite absent from the takeoff of an aeroplane. Why is this? Perhaps it is the slowness, the huge solemn noises, together with all the long associations of historical departures of emigration and empire. Tim and I walked back to AA with the certainty that life aboard would not be the same again. I tried to cheer him up. 'You'll have a lot more room in the aft cabin, and it will be healthier without all the cigarette smoke.' No reply.

Dave and Tim were now altogether out of danger from their poisoned legs, after a time of very disagreeable visits to the Papeete hospital. July 14th came and went in a crescendo of drumming, dancing, singing and boat racing. There seemed no reason for us to linger any longer in Tahiti. We had all become a little jaded, with a consequent lowering of morale. There was a scene in a waterside bar when Dave thumped an American for saying something disparaging about the Queen. I don't know what he said, but no one could possibly like being thumped by Dave so the offender left without delay. The celebrations had been fun, though I doubt if many Tahitians had much idea about the French Revolution.

The general consensus was that we had had enough Tahiti, so without any real regret we left for Moorea, seven miles to the northwest. Just before we sailed it rained heavily and Papeete steamed in the hot sun as we moved away from our berth, hauling up the anchor as we went. The mountains, wreathed in mists, loomed dramatically behind the town – it was typical of Tahiti to caricature itself in this way. It is – was – a place where the expected is what reveals itself. The only surprise was to find how completely the Chinese had taken over the commercial life, just as the Indians had taken over business in Fiji. The Polynesians seemed not to resent this; they were most good-natured and I could detect no rivalry at an entrepreneurial level.

Moorea was preferred by all of us, I think. It turned out to be unspoilt and delightful – the tropical paradise that Tahiti had no doubt once been, a dream island with towering peaks. Dave wanted to level them off, build a theme park, holiday camp and yacht marina, then finish tidying up the place by filling in the caves. He'd have been very enthusiastic about Disneyland if it had been invented then. An ideal Polynesian village among the palm trees was visible from our deck.

We anchored in the bay and set about preparing AA for her last long passage to Rarotonga and Auckland. As there was no opportunity to slip AA, we had to take her bottom on trust – in fact we preferred not to think about it. As for the leak, the general opinion was that water was coming in from several different sources, but it was not much and did not cause serious worry. Dave still pumped the deck pump for exercise when he felt like it, but there was no sense of urgency about what had become a recreational activity. As for our sailing gear, it had stood up remarkably well to wear and tear and it seemed that I had been unnecessarily pessimistic about chafe. George said that I was still under the delusion that AA was a yacht: 'You're like someone riding a carthorse who thinks he's on a hunter.' Although we had filled our fuel tanks in Papeete, we couldn't be certain that we would be able to reach Auckland without some help from the sails. We wanted to avoid having to buy more diesel in Rarotonga because it would be not only expensive but also awkward to get aboard. In normal circumstances we would burn 85 gallons a day, but how could we tell that circumstances would be normal? If, for example, we encountered strong headwinds all the way from Rarotonga to New Zealand, fuel would burn faster and we would travel more slowly. Pam and Muriel thought there was enough food to keep us alive, on the most basic fare. All delicacies had gone including, I believe, all beer and spirits. I can recall only tins of pork, spam, rice and cornflakes as I stumbled about in the food hold – not a wholesome diet.

Dick was fairly confident about the engine. By this time, he was completely familiar with all its quirks and failings; I doubt if it had any surprises left for him to be infuriated by. It was already worn and tired before we started. Nobody knew how many hours it had run in its life – we'd done another 2,000 on top and were about to add some more. Looking back on the whole voyage it strikes me that Dick had more to worry about than anyone else. Les was not a worrier, Jim knew exactly what he was doing and where we were, but that didn't include the engine room, while my sails were straightforward. Dick had to face the continual possibility of disaster, dealing with an engine of whose history he knew nothing – no record of maintenance, hours run, overhauls... Already fourteen years old when he first saw it lurking at the bottom of the engine room ladder, it must have been a formidable challenge – though of course he never said so. So far he had been able to start it and keep it running. I think we all felt a lift of the spirits whenever he opened the valve of the air bottles that started the brute, and heard it thump into life. Relief, too, but I'm not sure Jim shared that relief. He was like the centurion in the Bible – he was a professional. He assumed it would start, and would have been incredulous if it hadn't.

Jim and Dave went off on one of their long hikes into the interior. Apart from wandering around in the village, I was idle once I'd seen to the sails and cordage. I remember sitting on deck and admiring the dramatic skyscape silhouetted against the setting sun. Bill was there, we were drinking coffee and conversing with Muriel in the galley through the open scuttle. It was all very peaceful.

By this time we had pretty well run out of reading matter. All the paperbacks had disintegrated. I had read all my precious hardbacks, except one, which I had been keeping for this foreseen emergency. This was my copy of *Emma*, in the 1909 edition by Dent, with illustrations by C. E. Brock. I have it still, discoloured and battered, a stout little edition rather portentously named 'The Series of English Idylls', held together by a good leather binding on the spine. It was at Moorea that I embarked on my fourth reading of this extraordinary novel. It seemed appropriate that I should open it again here in Paopao Bay: the overwhelmingly dramatic scenery needed a powerful plot to compete with it – and that *Emma* certainly has. It continually reveals new delights, expanding in the mind to take up much more space there than is apparent on the page. I had not lent it to George because I did not want to hear him tell me that Emma was a snob.

* * * * *

We stayed at Moorea until July 24th – four days – then with Jim and Dave back on board after their expedition, weighed anchor and left for Rarotonga, rather more than 700 miles to the southwest. These anchor weighings were becoming a test of our trawling gear – Dave's department. How many more weighings could we depend on? From the expression on Dave's face as he stood at the controls, I thought not many. As it was with the engine, so it was with the trawl winch – we had no idea how much it had been used or when, if ever, it had been overhauled.

Once clear of Moorea, we set our rig, the trade wind still favouring us, and settled on our course to Rarotonga. It was a strange passage; some of the life seemed to have gone out of AA with the departure of Nigel and John. It is difficult to describe this. Life on board a boat builds up a rhythm, and routine, of its own which depends largely on the personalities of the crew, the daily exchanges. If two of the people concerned are missing it upsets the balance and there is a mild sense of dislocation. I found that I missed the badinage with Nigel, when I would disparage all things Australian and he would inveigh against everything English. John was usually with Nigel – they had become inseparable – so these exchanges were unfairly loaded against me. I learnt a great many Australian words and phrases – 'pie cruncher' and 'boof head' have stuck in my mind, among others. Because he was a fair-minded fellow John would sometimes take my side, but it was very hard to get the better of Nigel: he had an unerring instinct for the last word. Although our tea parties were no more, George and I would still sit on our deck chairs and talk. He was still able to dredge up some stories of his naval days that I had not heard. Many of them involved service on destroyers – extraordinary manoeuvres at very high speed: 'The skipper would lay his career on the line – you could hardly believe the risks he took with that ship.' I would look over the side at the sea moving past at about five knots and say, 'Wow – d'you mean faster than this?'

On the fifth day out from Moorea Rarotonga was sighted, under its cloud. By this time we were able to avoid irritating Jim with expressions of surprise. Rarotonga is round, with a volcano in the middle. I knew of it only what I had read in *Deep Water and Shoal*. Robinson had not been impressed with the government of the Cook Islands, administered by New Zealand. To him Rarotonga looked 'like the island of a pirate king' – not, I confess, a thought that occurred to me. He was scathing about the way the New Zealanders dealt with the place: 'This country has made the worst possible mess of governing its islands.' This was, of course, thirty years before our visit and no doubt there had been much improvement, but certainly the New Zealanders believed in bureaucracy. As we lay off the tiny entry 'port', a launch appeared carrying a pilot, a doctor and another official of indeterminate purpose. This was not at all what we had become accustomed to. I could see that Les was thinking hard and fast how he could avoid paying harbour and pilotage dues, perhaps even medical fees. They looked expensive, these people, in white shirts, shorts, and long white socks. We'd never seen anything like it. They all went up into the wheelhouse. As I was busy making the anchor ready for dropping I wasn't able to hear any of the conversation, but somehow Les managed to get rid of them at very little cost. Whatever he said to them, we had to admire his cheek.

The anchorage to which we were directed lay in a narrow channel between coral reefs, where we were to anchor, taking a line ashore to the jetty so that we wouldn't swing onto the coral. We needed, in effect, to be pinned down. We dropped anchor on a short scope of chain, then I set off for the jetty, with Bill in the stern of the dinghy to deal with the warp. It was the longest line that we possessed, thick and heavy to handle. George payed it out to us from the stern of AA, Bill having taken a turn with the free end round the aft thwart of the dinghy. It was hard rowing with a cross wind to contend with, added to which, before we reached the jetty, it became apparent that the warp was not long enough. There was not time for George to find another line to join it to, so the obvious manoeuvre was to slack the anchor chain thus allowing AA to drop back. This involved starting the engine again so that Dave could operate the trawl winch. The jetty, meanwhile, had become crowded with Rarotongans shouting encouragement as I toiled on the oars. This struggle was going to make their day. Dave slacked the chain, and AA started to drop back as planned. I thought one mighty effort would do it and put all my weight into the oars, with the consequence that one of them broke (they were worn where they had chafed in the rowlocks – like practically everything on AA they should have been replaced). The dinghy spun round.

A cheer went up from the assembled audience as I was obliged to scull back to AA with one oar over the transom. Meanwhile of course, AA was on a longer scope of anchor chain so she was swinging perilously close to the coral. Luckily Dick saw the impending danger and gave her a quick burst forward to straighten her up, while Dave took in the chain on the winch. We were back where we had started. We attached another length to the warp, I took one of the longboat oars as a replacement for the broken one, and we set off to have another go. The longboat oar was too long and too thick so that it tried to jam in the rowlock. After furious struggles I managed to reach the jetty and make fast to a bollard, to the disappointment of the Rarotongans, who were having a splendid time. As I came alongside AA again, Jim was leaning over the bulwark: 'Wasn't rowing on the curriculum at Pangbourne, then?' he asked. I was glad that Nigel hadn't been there to witness the exhibition. These exertions required a rest in my cabin until teatime. The trouble with life afloat is that there are so many things to go wrong, and anything that can, will.

The next day we went ashore to buy fresh food. We found bananas, oranges and coconuts, all very cheap. Nobody felt inclined to climb the 3,000-foot peak in the middle of the island, but Bill and I went for a walk on the flat, along the road that ran around the coast. 'Only another 1,300 miles,' he said, as we stared out towards New Zealand to the southwest. There was evidence of the tidal wave on Rarotonga, while oddly there had been none on Tahiti. I do not understand how a tidal wave sweeping across the Pacific could miss some places out while doing considerable damage in others. There is much mystery in the world of oceanography. Why, for example, are some waves in a series much bigger than the others? Anyone who has spent time at sea will have noticed this, but I've never heard a convincing explanation.

It was not easy to get away from Rarotonga on August 1st. Our 112 lb plough anchor had nestled firmly down into a coral cave, a wonderful holding position but not one which would allow removal by any obvious means. Dave started up the anchor winch and hauled in the chain until it was straight up and down, but the CQR wouldn't come out of its hole. We could see all this by leaning over the bow. We drove AA backwards and forwards, to no avail, getting crosser and sweatier, and nearly came to the conclusion that we would have to leave anchor and chain as a parting present to the Rarotongans. But no, there had to be one last attempt. Half an hour later, after circling the anchor, pulling at it from several different directions in turn, tugging and wrenching, it came away, and we were off. I found that the anchor shank had twisted through about fifty degrees: it was as if two giant hands had gripped it to give it a sharp turn. But at least we still had it.

At last we were headed direct to Auckland, 1,300 miles away. I stowed away the sails – we wouldn't be needing them again, except for the mizzen, sheeted hard in. The wind soon became westerly, coming straight out of the Tasman sea and gaining in strength as we proceeded – sitting on deck was a thing of the past. But that was the least of our worries. Jim became ill. The chief symptom was a very high temperature. He moved to Nigel's old bunk in the aft cabin, where there was less motion and where Muriel could keep an eye on him. There he lay, quietly on his back, like a crusading knight on his tomb. He ate nothing. It was hard for Muriel, trying to nurse him without any drugs or equipment. AA was filled with gloom – his fever was too high for safety; there was a period when I think it must have occurred to many of us that Jim might die. It was unthinkable, but it certainly crossed my mind. Dave was particularly upset as he and Jim had become close friends.

We became accustomed to the continual headwinds

with the succession of great rollers on their way around the bottom of the world, as we smashed slowly towards Auckland. There was something majestic about this wilderness of water, and in no way did our situation seem comparable to the hysterical hurricane in Biscay. AA chuntered on at about half throttle and at intervals of about half a minute she would thump into a roller. This would bring her to a standstill before she moved slowly forward again. We would come off watch, go down to the aft cabin to look at Jim, then turn in until it was time to do something about food. I continued sleeping in the fo'c'sle; by this time I hardly noticed the up-and-down swooping that had caused such odd dreams earlier. Sometimes, as AA crashed into a big one, it felt, where I was lying up forward, as if she had run into a pile of bricks, but I barely noticed. I think we were all getting a little daft. I was reading *Emma* and had got it into my head that Harriet was the natural daughter of Mr Knightley and I was the first person in the world to think of this; I was very pleased with my 'discovery'. The stove was lit in the aft cabin, where we would huddle to eat our horrid meals and tell each other what we were going to do when we reached Auckland. A ditty kept going round and round in my head: 'As I was sitting by O'Reilly's fire, drinking O'Reilly's rum and water.' Keeping dry was a problem. My only pair of oilskin trousers had been cut to destruction when I sat on the shards of glass lying on the chart table many months earlier; once my jeans were soaked with salt water, they stayed soaked.

The only land that we were in the least likely to see on our way were the Kermadec Islands, to the north of our course. They are no more than islets, with a total area of hardly more than a dozen square miles, uninhabited except for a weather station on the largest in the group. We weren't seriously afraid of running into them, but there was always the sneaking fear, in my mind anyway, that we might be off course – we hadn't been able to take sights for days – and I was always aware of the Diego Ramirez factor. Jim's illness made us rather short of navigational expertise: we had always depended on him to tell us precisely where we were.

After about a week – and at this period of the voyage the days and nights had become shapeless, running into each other in a confusing manner – Jim started to recover. As soon as Muriel allowed him, he appeared on deck, sitting wraithlike on the aft grating. 'Where are we?' he asked. 'I don't know, we're all waiting for you to tell us,' I said. He had hardly been on deck for an hour or so when there was a gleam of sunshine. Sights could be taken, and it was established that we were barely three days from Auckland.

Those weary last three days! We were all aching to get to New Zealand; the passage from Rarotonga was beginning to seem intolerably long. On August 14th we sighted Great Barrier Island and stared at it almost unbelievingly – this was a piece of actual New Zealand – then we moved slowly into the Haurake Gulf. As we came into Auckland harbour, we passed an Ellerman liner, the *City of Edinburgh*, belching coal smoke in the dock. She seemed huge. We tied up close to the ferry boat dock and waited for Customs clearance. We'd made it.

* * * * *

This story does not have an altogether happy ending. The whole intention of taking AA to New Zealand had been to sell her at a profit to the Wellington Fishermen's Cooperative, to use for fishing for blue cod in the Chatham Islands. She did indeed come under offer to them shortly after her arrival, subject to survey for condition. Those dreadful words! My experience as a yacht broker had taught me how a survey for condition could bring the most auspicious sale crashing to the ground. An ill-founded optimism had led me to suppose that this wouldn't be the case with *Aberdeen Anzac*, and I hardly need to add that I was quite wrong. When she was slipped at Auckland it was found that her bottom was riddled with teredo worm, very probably picked up while we were lying close to wooden pilings in Papeete. Looking at her on the slip I saw the worms for myself. Fat creatures, they were, that had inserted themselves into the bottom planking, then eaten their way along the grain of the wood. In short, her bottom was nearly porous and she had to be replanked. As one might imagine, the cost of this absorbed nearly all the profit from the sale. She also had to be re-engined, not so much because her existing unit was worn out — maybe it just needed an overhaul — but because it was not powerful enough for her new work. It was removed and replaced with another of double the horsepower. I understood that AA would have to 'tow whales' in future, in addition to fishing for blue cod. I have no idea what she eventually did; I have never seen her again or heard any news of her.

Her crew scattered. Jim and Dave rented an apartment outside Auckland. Jim found a job in a shipping office where, when I went to see him, he was at a desk pushing papers around, looking hunched in a collar and tie. Dave eventually went back to sea, and I remember the last thing he said to me was that the New Zealanders really ought to have more originality than to call their two islands North Island and South Island. Dick found work with a local tycoon looking after his fine yacht. Bill, Tim and I lived in the Sailors' Home for a time and worked for the Ferguson Tractor Company, putting up Dexion shelving in their spare-parts warehouse. Muriel and George went off to find teaching jobs. Once AA was sold, Les and Pam left for a tour of New Zealand.

Back in England the following year, Jim and I had dinner together. He had just been given command of a small freighter to take out to New Zealand. There were a number of things wrong with it but, as I told him, it would be luxury compared to *Aberdeen Anzac*. In 1962 Dave came to stay the weekend with my wife and me. He had by then made another trip to Auckland in another trawler – a much better organised operation in a better-found vessel. We have seen Tim quite often since he returned to his home in Margate. Nigel and his wife Jean, and John, have been to see us, but very sadly Nigel died several years ago. I saw Les once, in 1961, before he returned to Australia. Pam came back to England and married; we have seen her quite recently. I lost track of Dick and Bill quite soon. We are all getting old.

The voyage of the *Aberdeen Anzac* had been a strange interlude (and I am aware that strictly speaking, a voyage should include return to the point of departure; what we had done had been a passage). When I think about it now, it occurs to me that if Jim had not been with us we might not have reached our destination. Nobody else was a competent navigator. He was not on the original crew list, he just happened to be in Southwick and as I explained, he came aboard out of curiosity, then asked if he could join. He was, I suppose, a sort of *deus ex machina*, placed on AA for our safety. Thinking of Jim, he seems an improbable guardian angel, but no doubt they take unusual and surprising forms. That, then, is our story. I'm glad I took part.

GLOSSARY

The nautical vocabulary is a living language, changing through the decades and reflecting the developing technology of navigation and seamanship. The words and phrases used forty to fifty years ago are, in many cases, now obsolete, but I have been obliged to use them because they were used at the time and there are no satisfactory substitutes. To save the reader the tedious trouble of looking them up in a dictionary – and they are not always there – I have listed below those that I think may now present difficulty. My apologies to those to whom such words as 'baggy-wrinkle' are well known.

Baggy-wrinkle A bushy coat of teased-out rope strands, attached to wire stays to prevent chafe.

Beaufort scale A scale of wind strengths, devised by Admiral Sir Francis Beaufort (1774–1857), ranging from 0 to 12, indicating flat calm up to a hurricane.

Belaying pins The pins, made either of wood or steel, which fit into a fife rail, onto which lines can be belayed, or made fast. The belaying pin played a large part in enforcing marine discipline in sailing ship days, being used as a weapon by mates and petty officers. The verb, to belay, meant shut up or stop doing what you are doing, as well as the proper meaning of taking a turn round a pin or cleat.

Bobstay A wire or chain stay running from the forefoot of a boat to the end of the bowsprit to counter the pull of the forestay.

Bilges The lowest part of the hull, in which water and any other liquid collects.

Bolt-rope Rope sewn round the edges of a sail to prevent it from tearing and to maintain its shape.

Bulwarks The raised woodwork surrounding a deck to keep the sea off: in the case of AA about two feet high.

Chronometer A very accurate timepiece, with compensating mechanism to counteract climatic conditions, used to determine longitude in celestial navigation.

CQR A plough-shaped anchor.

Dead reckoning Navigation based only on a ship's course and speed, without benefit of celestial observation. Used in overcast conditions and not reliable over long distances.

Elsan Chemical toilet.

Eye bolt A bolt with an eye in it to take a hook or ring.

Fiddle A raised wooden ridge around a cabin table or working surface to stop things rolling onto the cabin sole.

Fife rail A wooden rail designed to hold belaying pins, which are removable. Two fife rails were made by Nigel, inside the port and starboard bulwarks.

Founder To sink.

Gaff Two meanings: (1) a spar aloft, holding up a four-sided sail; and (2) a pole with a large hook on the end to lift fish straight out of the water.

Great circle The shortest distance between two positions on a globe. This is shown as a curve on a Mercator projection, as in an atlas.

Gringo A mildly pejorative name for an American, used by Latin Americans.

Ground tackle Anchors and chain.

Kicking strap Similar to a boom vang. A line used to stop a boom from lifting up, spilling wind.

Luff On AA it meant the fore edge of a sail, the other meaning as a verb having no relevance to her.

Lazarette A space between decks on a merchant vessel, used as a store room.

Manilla A type of rope, named after the capital of the Philippines.

Monkey's fist A large tight knot at the end of a heaving line, giving weight.

Nobbie A type of traditional Lancashire fishing boat.

Pipe cot A bunk made from a surrounding metal pipe onto which is laced a canvas sheet. This can be surprisingly comfortable because with time the canvas accommodates the body shape of the sleeper.

Scuppers The drains running round the outer edge of the deck; the general drainage area to take water off the deck.

Scowegian A general term for Scandinavians.

Scuttle The same thing as a port hole, or if there is a difference I am ignorant of it.

Servings Thin lines wound round splices to make them neat and, in the case of wire, to prevent them developing spikes which would make them hard to handle.

Sheave A block designed to take wire rope.

Shrouds The wire or ropes supporting the mast by being attached to the ship's side.

Splice Various forms of treatment of ropes and wire. The well-known ones are eye splices (to put an eye into a rope), back splice (to make a neat end to a rope and prevent it from fraying) and a long splice (to join two lengths of rope together end to end).

Tabernacle A support for the heel of a mast, when it is stepped on deck.

Thimble A metal eye, spliced into the end of a rope, usually to take a shackle or hook. It prevents the rope from fraying.

Ticket Short for Master's Certificate. A Board of Trade qualification allowing a deck officer to command a ship. It is gained by examination, following earlier exams for Second Mate and Mate. It is a stiff exam, but there is an even stiffer one for Extra Masters.

Warp A large rope for mooring boats or for towing and other heavy work.

This list is by no means exhaustive. We tended to use nautical terms only when necessary, because the great majority of us were not sailors. Jim used Merchant Navy expressions from habit, some of which were not those used by yachtsmen. For example, he would refer to 'breaking out', say, some previously unused food tins from the lazarette. George used Royal Navy expressions, also from habit. Sometimes his remarks could be unintelligible and I had to learn what 'three badgers' and 'nutty' meant. A complete lexicon of sea language through the ages would be a fat volume.

POSTSCRIPT – 2005

Aberdeen Anzac was something of a mystery ship, with a great gap in her history. According to the details given in the particulars printed by the East Coast Yacht Agency when she was offered for sale in 1959, she had been built by G. Forbes of Peterhead in 1946. These details were described as 'Provisional', which suggests to me that we were not very confident of their accuracy and hoped to find out more in due course. Although we all thought of her as an 'Admiralty' MFV (Motor Fishing Vessel), we never had any evidence of Admiralty use.

She was constructed of larch planking on oak frames with galvanised iron fastenings. The larch may have contributed to her attractiveness to the teredo worms which attacked her in the Pacific. Her dimensions were 70 feet overall, 65 feet on the waterline, a beam of 19 feet and draught of 9 feet. She was fitted with a well-used seine net winch and coiler, and it was claimed that her mizzen mast, together with its tabernacle, had been 'just fitted'. That did not, of course, mean that it was new. Yacht brokers are careful about their claims concerning craft they offer for sale, not wanting to be in trouble for misrepresentation. We at the East Coast Yacht Agency used to print on our detail sheets 'the particulars given are believed to be accurate, but are not guaranteed, and buyers should satisfy themselves regarding same.' Her engine was a typical 160-horsepower Lister Blackstone diesel engine, started by compressed air in bottles. A speed of 8.5 knots was claimed for her, but nobody believed that – she never achieved more than 7 knots while we were in her. She might possibly have managed a little more, but Dick was certainly not going to try and find out. He had to nurse that engine for more than 12,000 miles. She reached 7 knots in the Panama Canal, briefly, because that was the regulation minimum speed, but she blew a gasket, making Dick more stony-faced than usual. Five knots was our usual gait. None of us was interested in her past or her provenance, being concerned only with what she could do for us and whether she would hold together until we reached Auckland. In the event, she proved to be a fine sea boat in spite of her uncomfortable motion. Her personality – and all boats have a personality – was tough, obdurate and reassuring. We grew fond of her, crediting her with a character which we hoped would see us through to the end. It did.

Several things, some of them melancholy, have happened to the crew since I completed this account. Nigel's wife, Jean, did not long survive him, dying in Queensland at the end of 2000, and at about the same time Tim died, on the very day that the manuscript of this story thumped through his letterbox in Margate. He had been to visit us several times over the years, including sometimes for Christmas. His memory was a useful aid to my own, providing me with details of things which had faded in my recollection. We miss him. Dick, stirred by this book, has emerged from a long silence and we correspond, sending each other calendars with pictures of New Zealand from him and Suffolk from us. He is much less laconic on paper than he was in speech. He has led a wandering life, but has come to rest with his family near Auckland, not far from our biggest asset, Jim.

Last year my wife and I went to see Dave, who lives with his wife Helen on a narrowboat on the Grand Union Canal, having retired to England after many years in New Zealand. I asked him if he had any news of *Aberdeen Anzac*, and he told me that she had been wrecked off the coast of South Island many years ago. She was a total loss, but no one was drowned.

C. A. LATIMER

C. A. Latimer was born in 1929 to a family of journalists on his father's side and flour and biscuit manufacturers on his mother's, neither of which would explain his interest in all forms of ship and boat – from rusty Thames lighters to huge ocean liners. This interest led to an education at the Nautical College, Pangbourne, where he failed eyesight tests for both Royal and Merchant navies. Conscripted into the army, he was fortunate to find himself in charge of unloading salt from Sunderland flying boats during the Berlin Airlift of 1948–49, with a team of stevedores from the Berlin docks and a fine fleet of tugs and pontoons to look after. After demob he worked in the family milling business, sailing frequently in Ivan Carr's exquisite *Solway Maid*, last-built of William Fife III's creations. He left to become a yacht broker with the East Coast Yacht Agency (subsequently Interyacht) in Woodbridge, Suffolk, before setting off in *Aberdeen Anzac* for New Zealand. On his way back he married his wife Sarah in Princeton, New Jersey, then settled in Woodbridge again, working at Interyacht until retirement. *Solway Maid* had rather spoilt him for other yachts, but he was able to transfer his affections to *Aberdeen Anzac*, recognising her splendid, if un-yachtlike, qualities.

MAP OF PASSAGE TO AUCKLAND

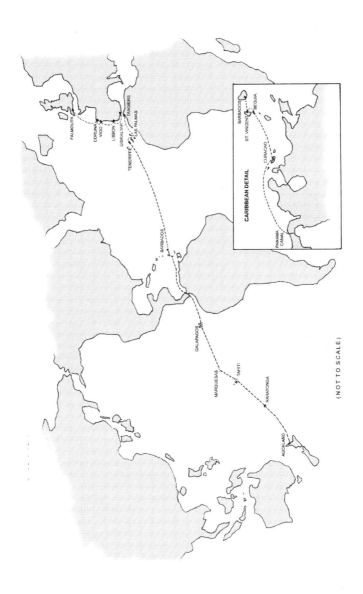